EXECUTE TO SUCCEED

Learn How to Make Your Business Consistently Profitability...FAST!

Ron Vest

Execute to Succeed Copyright © 2017 by Ron Vest. All Rights Reserved.

All rights reserved. No part of this book may be reproduced in any form or by any electronic or mechanical means including information storage and retrieval systems, without permission in writing from the author. The only exception is by a reviewer, who may quote short excerpts in a review.

Cover designed by Ron Vest

This book is a work of fiction. Names, characters, places, and incidents either are products of the author's imagination or are used fictitiously. Any resemblance to actual persons, living or dead, events, or locales is entirely coincidental.

Ron Vest
Visit my website at AFSProfit.com
Visit me on Facebook at facebook.com/smallbusinesschamp/

Printed in the United States of America

First Printing: Dec 2017
createspace

ISBN-13:
978-1979477314

ISBN-10:
1979477310

CONTENTS

Forward 1
part one 4
Chapter 1 5
    What is a revenue leak? 5
Chapter 2 7
    Revenue Leaks in Action and its affect on profit 7
    Profit, a Contradiction 9
    What should you do? 10
    Let's begin with Profit 10
Chapter 3 14
    Where to begin? 14
    At certain times it is foolish to act quickly 14
    Create your future in Five Steps 16
Chapter 4 20
    It all begins with the Customer 20
    Just who is your customer? 21
    How to develop a customer profile 22
Chapter 5 24
    And Now, Marketing 24
    Mastering Core Marketing Principles 25
    Positioning is first 25

Packaging is second 25
Promotion is third 26
Persuasion is fourth 26
Performance comes last 27
Building a 5P Marketing Plan 27
Positioning your business 28
Packaging your services 28
Promoting your services 29
The persuasion process 30
Performance in your company 31
A nine-step sales process that leads to success 33

Chapter 6 35
The Role of Branding 35
How branding can increase your profits 35
Can branding make you more money? 37
Do you really need a branding strategy? 39

Chapter 7 42
Pricing and Value 42
Are you currently getting value from your pricing? 43
Price is what you pay, But value is what you get 46

Chapter 8 48
How to balance the value formula 48
Tilting the value balance in your favor 51

Chapter 9 55
Do you really know your costs? 55
How you can make pinning the tail on the donkey more accurate ... 55
Are you stumbling in the dark with your actual cost of labor? 57

Chapter 10 61
revenue Leaking Processes 61

The processes by which you operate your company 62
Market Related Processes 64
Chapter 11 67
How to Grow your Business 67
The Right Way to Grow Your Business 70
Avoiding Cash Flow Perils 74
Chapter 12 79
Measurement and Management – We cannot manage what we do not measure!
.... 79
Do you report to yourself each month? 80
What KPI's might you include in your monthly report? 82
Performance also counts! 83
Efficiency 86
Where would your company be without customers? 87
Without having measurements there can be no improvement 89
Chapter 13 92
Benchmarking 92
Does your business stack up against the industry? 93
part TWO 96
Forward 97
Chapter 14 98
Accounting Fundamentals 98
Double-entry System 98
Types of General Ledger Accounts 99
External Financial Statements 99
Chapter 15 101
Accounting Standards 101
Bookkeeping 102
Profit and Loss 103

Chapter 16 104
Bookkeeping: Fundamental Principles 104
Making a Profit 105
Assets and Liabilities 106
Gains and Losses 107
Balance Sheet 107
Revenue and Receivables 108
Inventory and Expenses 109
Depreciation 110
Depreciation Reporting 110
Investing and Financing 111
Building Cash Reserves 112

Chapter 17 114
Managing the Bottom Line 114
Exactly what is the FASB? 115
What Exactly are Auditors? 116
What exactly is Forensic Accounting? 117
Who uses forensic accountants? 118
What is the Sarbanes-Oxley Act? 118
What happened at Enron? 119
What Happens in a Corporate Accounting Scandal? 120
Disclosure 121
What's Financial Window Dressing? 122
What is a Corporation? 123
What are Partnerships and Limited Liability Companies? 124
What is a Sole Proprietorship? 125
Budgeting 126
Regarding GAAP 126
Categories of Costs 127

- The Importance of Measuring Costs 128
- The Components of an Income Statement 129
- Tips on how to analyze a financial statement 131
- Just what are Earnings Per Share? 132
- Understanding price/earnings ratio 133
- What's the Difference Between Public and Private Organization Reporting? . 133
- What are Additional Ratios Utilized in Financial Reporting? 134
- Discover the Acid Test Ratio and ROA Ratio. 135
- What exactly are Independent Auditors? 136
- What do they mean by Accounting Fraud? 137
- What is the Purpose of an Audit? 138
- What Does an Audit Report Contain? 139
- How Accounting is Used in Business? 139

Some additional tools to help you. 141
- Forensic Diagnostic 141
- Dashboard Monthly Report 141
- SLIGHT CHANGES = Big Results - How to Dramatically Improve your Quotes & Proposals 142
- 10 Tools to Increase Sales 143

About ron vest 144

This book is dedicated to my wife, Angie, whose accomplishments, drive, and determination, have proven that if you have a dream you believe in you can achieve it. With all my Love

"Strategy is a commodity, execution is an art."

—PETER DRUCKER

FORWARD

This book is comprised of two sections. The first section discusses profitability. Some people only think of increasing sales to increase profitability, but it is so much more. If you increase sales but your true cost of sales is higher than you are aware of you may lose money on each sale. You also have to be aware of the management of people, process's, as well as expense structure. This, plus more, is what we will review in the profitability section. The second section gives you the fundamentals of accounting. *Don't skip this section!* When I was in school I hated math. When I discovered how it can help immensely in uncovering hidden profits and areas of opportunities I became very interested. Reading and understanding this section will allow you to have a deeper understanding of your business, help you to make more profit, and become a significant resource to assist you in fighting fraud and theft within your company.

Executing the concepts below are meant to considerably increase your profits.

That doesn't mean it's achieved without working hard and having diligence while keeping in mind that hope and intention is not a strategy. The principles have to be applied.

They develop from being hands-on, engaging in the operations forensics and dealing with owners, executive management, and supervisors, to find and stop profit leaks. Clients get in touch with me when they're just simply unsatisfied with the way their own company is progressing. Insufficient cash in the bank as well as the lifestyle which leads to (among other things); feeling annoyed, stressed, too little time to consider long-term, inadequate time for the family, and never enough time to enjoy pleasure in their life.

By using these tips, I have continually been able to uncover a number of improvements. Improvements which stop profit leaks, put money in the bank, and result in a better business and way of life. It's not brain surgery, but it's what I do. Because I've been doing this for quite a while, I've discovered ways to determine where the leak may be and 'solve the mystery'. You are doing the same thing within your company because you're great at what you do.

The image I plan to present is that potential profits within your company that may be slipping away but that, if stopped and accumulated, can make an impressive impact on the cash in your bank as well as your overall profitability.

This book is about being aware of what a revenue leak is and exactly where to watch out for them in a business. Why is that significant? Ultimately, it's about cash flow, and the independence that it provides.

These profit leaks stopgap tips aren't theoretical. They're realistic, built upon over twenty-five years of working together, and for, small business owners to help them recognize those areas of their company which are draining their profits, and to develop methods to stop the leak and assemble a far better business.

Those enhancements have more than doubled a number of client's profits and lead to more substantial growth in others.

Obviously, I don't understand your business as well as you do; nobody does, and it also would be presumptuous of me to suggest otherwise. What I do provide is expertise in particular techniques and process's that can be implemented widely to all small business.

This book is about comprehending what a revenue leak is, where you can look for them in a company and the impact it'll have on your own business with regards to the availability of cash, profits, and chosen lifestyle.

I want to see small business owners develop in their business to ensure that they become financial managers, not simply selling managers. I don't mean that in condescending manner. I want to see them take control of their company, to ensure that they control their business rather than it controlling them.

I want to see all of them be successful, be extremely profitable, to not be continually worried about money, to achieve the lifestyle they really want, never to feel they must spend every single waking hour in their business.

So, what is required to achieve this?

1. Measurement. However, it has to be the measurement of the correct things, the ones that enable small business owners to identify revenue leaks and inform on their improvement.

2. Reporting systems that gather and present the data easily. If it's too hard to collect, they won't report on it.

3. Written reporting - reports have to be written. It's only in writing the reports that they're more likely to take into account the consequences of them.

4. Why is this? All reports should have a "Why is this?" section. Without having that they are less inclined to analyze and understand what is taking place in their business.

5. Benchmarking - can they improve? Benchmarking can reveal further opportunities which the owner or manager may not be aware. Benchmarking can be advantageous whether you compare against "like" companies or your own information. Choose wisely though.

6. Step-by-step improvement - it's difficult to attempt to change everything at the same time, plus much more likely to lead to just giving up. Modest improvements will demonstrate results and encourage them to keep improving.

My personal strategy is to attempt to throw some light on the dark recesses of your small business where the profit losing enemies lurk. Take action. Read the whole book, select just a few techniques, try them, and measure the after and before results. Rinse and repeat. You will definitely get results.

PART ONE

Operations Profitability

CHAPTER 1

WHAT IS A REVENUE LEAK?

I'm glad you asked! Allow me to recall an issue a friend of mine had a while ago with his water bill. Where he had lived for 30 years, is in the tropics. So, he basically had two seasons the wet season and the dry season. Through the dry season he might go for 5-6 months without even a drop of rain, however the weather conditions more than makes up for it during the wet season.

A tropical storm can be a wonder to behold, imposing thunderheads, amazing lightening. Where he lived allegedly has more lightning strikes every year than any other location, anywhere. NASA has even sent unique airplanes to study the phenomenon.

Since there is no rain throughout the dry season (of course) when you've got a garden you must water it. Most people there install automated sprinklers. Therefore, the reverse applies during the wet season, and so they turn their sprinklers off. Be patient with me, I'm getting there.

They're billed quarterly for their water. If they had been billed month-to-month my friend likely would have noticed the problem earlier. (Hint - that's why you have to review your accounts along with other KPI's (key performance indicators) on at least a month-to-month basis.) It was a wet season bill, and the bill was more than twice what he had been expecting. An extremely big OUCH! What had caused this?

There were no leaking faucets, or even dripping anywhere, in either the house or in the garden. Not even lush green areas. Being the wet season, the entire garden was lush and green. So where was the problem and how did he locate it?

In the end he discovered it accidentally walking into a very slushy part of the garden. Underneath the slushy part was a cracked pipe where all the water was coming from.

However, that was pure luck. I assume he would have found it eventually if he had completed a careful investigation. But finding leaks accidentally is just not good enough.

And that's the main problem you may have in your business. Occasionally the leaking faucet is pretty obvious. A specific product or activity is undoubtedly costing you money. If you're able to see it, you can do something about it. But what about the instances when you don't know you're having a revenue leak? You don't know until you receive the quarterly, or semiannual or, worse yet, the annual figures. Simply because at that point it's too late. The revenues have disappeared.

You might plug the leak, but what is gone is gone.

So maybe you should be a revenue leak investigator to identify the signs to a problem (AKA hidden leaks) and to put the revenue leak to rest.

Are there any areas of your company which aren't performing as well as they need to?

Are you in markets which don't perform as well as others you should be in?

Are their clients who are less than profitable?

Is a good performance in a single area of your company covering up a poor performance in another?

Are your profit margins what they ought to, or could, be?

Do you truly know your cost of sales? If you don't, I'd be willing to bet you aren't recouping all of those costs, and are writing them off against overhead, not regaining them against the sale.

So a revenue leak can occur in any area of your company, whether it be marketing and advertising, sales, purchasing, or admin. It may be a system or process, poor accounting or expense control. The main factor is that it is happening out of sight, and being out of sight, no-one is doing anything about it.

Revenues that leak are gone permanently. That's why they must be hunted down and fixed.

CHAPTER 2

REVENUE LEAKS IN ACTION AND ITS AFFECT ON PROFIT

So what is more essential, cash flow or profit?
The perils associated with profitless cash flow!
A number of events brought up this question which I thought worth discussing right up front. The first was a remark concerning the very concept of revenue leaks, and the second a scenario I discovered where, despite an enormous and very visible leak, the company wanted to maintain the unprofitable operations for the cash they bought in.

The remark was that profit is an inadequate word because profit is a subjective number. It is actually true that the profit of virtually any business bigger than a teenager's babysitting service or a newspaper delivery route is impacted by a number of arbitrary allocations and decisions that you might make, or that your accountant may "creatively" make.

As an example, when you run an advertising campaign, is 100% of the cost an immediate expenditure or would you allocate the cost over a longer timeframe because it produces lasting value? Your final decision affects your profit number.

All of that is quite true. You can do either. It's tough to dispute the facts.

The individual that made the remark then continued to extol the benefits of cash. "Cash is real. That advertising campaign has to be paid as it occurs and the expense of it is immediate cash out of pocket."

Losing cash is worse than a revenue leak! Well, kind of. I learned a long time ago that cash flow is king. You can't pay bills without cash, no matter how profitable your company is.

But there's an inherent challenge in considering cash as being more essential than profit in the long term.

So, let's take a look at the second event, a real-life situation, to see the reason why. Real life situations are a lot better than theoretical examples with regards to illustrating a point.

The real-life situation is a company with many small profit centers. Even though the company is profitable overall, around 70% of the small profit centers were losing money. Is that a revenue leak or what?! A quick check implied most of these would have to increase sales by greater than 31% to break even, with one needing to improve by more than 118%. That sounds like hard work to me.

Perhaps increasing gross profit isn't as hard. So, I ran a 'what if' scenario on increasing gross profit. I'm a true believer in the power of gross profit, however that didn't help much either. A substantial lift in sales continued to be required.

If neither increasing sales, nor increasing gross profits, will improve the situation then perhaps the organization is much better off without those particular profit centers. "But we need the cash flow from them to pay the bills" I was told.

And it's true that the cash flow from these centers was more regular compared to the areas earning profits, so they always had cash coming in. I've witnessed it before, individuals hanging onto operations in spite of profitless cash flow.

However, cash coming in is all good but if a business is taking a leak, then with every turn of the working capital wheel a little is shaved off. You begin with $200, it goes around and comes back as $178, around again and you have $162.

It's not exactly the way to make you roll in funds. For that, you must have a margin on top that goes into your bank account. That is real cash.

Profit is essential to business. It is primeval. Profit is the reason why people are in business, to improve their monetary position. Quite a few cloak their profit motivation with a strong code of ethics; other people, regrettably, don't care about ethics. Some individuals use profits to fulfill a need for independence, freedom, or perhaps the desire to be one's own boss. Unless they generate a profit that leads to money in the bank, they can't accomplish any of these.

Show me someone in business who doesn't seek to generate a profit, you would be hard pressed to find one. At its most elementary, if they don't have profits, they don't have a business. Most small business people, the target market of my business, don't think in overly sophisticated terms like ROI (return on investment). For these people it's just PROFIT, never mind how the creative accountants may present it.

This isn't to minimize the significance of cash flow, but profitless cash flow is useless. In the Working Capital wheel, it doesn't take much to clog the wheel and get you in all types of difficulty financially.

To prevent that you need a margin on the cash flowing throughout the business that you could deposit into your bank account. The bigger the bank account the better off you are to endure that rainy day.

Let's discuss revenue leaks. Leakage is sinister. You don't know they're happening, but they are, at least in most small companies, and in most large companies for that matter. If it was a massive leak, water spraying everywhere, even the ineptest entrepreneur will see it as well as do something about it. It is the leakage that they don't see that sucks away the revenues. In the introduction to this book I illustrated the problem with a real-life metaphor concerning the cost of an unseen leak in a water pipe.

A great number of small business people are working their butts off simply to stay one-step ahead of their bills because they aren't aware of the profits they're losing. Not everyone is in this predicament. For some, they just really need to sell more.

P.S. There was an extremely happy conclusion to the above real-life situation. My client repaired the businesses leaking revenues, and grew the profitable side of the company, eliminating the leaks and retaining the revenues.

But revenue is invariably a paradox to small business owners.

PROFIT, A CONTRADICTION

Cash Flow is cash as well as a fact. Profit is an opinion, both a contradiction and an illusion.

Your books may convince you that your company is profitable; however, you can still go bankrupt because you don't have the cash.

However, a strong cash flow can be an illusion; a company can still go broke if it is profitless cash flow.

Insufficient cash is the primary issue facing so many small businesses today. It doesn't make a difference whether the company is taking its first preliminary steps, or has been running for many years, it still requires operating cash flow to cover the bills. Without readily available cash, businesses can go down in flames.

WHAT SHOULD YOU DO?

Even though cash is crucial, people think in terms of profits rather than cash. We all do. You seldom hear a business person speak about cash flow problems, they talk about profits. When you think about a startup business, an expansion, or any other investment, you think about the expense, what you could sell the product or service for, along with what the profits could be. We're trained to think of business in terms of profitability - as sales minus costs and expenses, i.e. profits.

Regrettably, we can't spend the profits directly. We spend the cash that sales generate. Profitable companies can go broke because they had almost all their money tied up in current, as well as fixed, assets and can't pay their bills. Cash flow and profit don't always match up.

LET'S BEGIN WITH PROFIT

Profit is the money left over once bills are paid. Some individuals think business owners can take profit home, but it's not that simple. Profit is necessary to pay for new equipment and the goods or materials necessary to run the business.

Only after paying for operations, and of course taxes, would you get to take money home.

Net profit is a great measure of the success of your company and, when compared to the investment made to create that profit, whether it was a worthwhile investment.

Which profit are we talking about though? It all depends on the factors applied.

The basic definition of net profit is revenue for that time period minus the expenses that allowed that revenue to be acquired during that time period. But the factors utilized, for example scheduling of expense accruals, the management of depreciation, computing the product or service's cost, allowances for bad debts etc. will affect the final number.

Also, if you don't understand or know the assumptions made for your business, you could be deceived about the results.

Here is another reason for possible confusion; a business doesn't have to collect from its clients to have incoming cash. Businesses frequently have an overdraft account to survive until revenue is available.

Which brings us to Cash Flow

Cash flow refers to the money coming in and going out of the business. Timing will become an issue. Frequently businesses spend money on wages, materials, products for resale etc., prior to bringing in any revenue.

There's two main forms of cash flow (actually there are more but we'll leave those to the accountants).

Operating cash flow is the outcome of any cash activity in a business's operations, whether or not the cash transaction is producing any earned revenue, or incurring expense, during the time of the transaction. For instance, clients may make advanced payments for future purchases, which increases cash holdings but doesn't have any effect on its presently reported profitability.

Then there's financing cash flow: the cash coming in as a result of the sale of property or equipment (fixed assets), or from purchasing property, fixtures, accessories or equipment. They aren't the result of the company's operating actions and therefore could be unrelated to its profitability. With that said, of course investing can result in an improved operation and enhance profitability, but the investment itself is not an expense and so not an aspect of the profitability calculation.

Likewise, obtainable cash can differ through taking out overdrafts or other loans and repaying them.

Financing activity is necessary and appropriate in particular situations, such as at start-up, growth or economic downturn recovery. Even so, excessive dependence on such capital inflows will ultimately result in business failure. Continual success is completely dependent on consistent, positive cash flow from business operations.

Profit does not equal cash flow in a company. Your company's Profit & Loss Report will show you if your business generated a profit or loss for the year, however it won't tell you anything concerning your cash flow. Your balance sheet will state your cash position (according to your bank statement) as well as where cash is tied up (inventory, debts, and Work-in-Progress). It will also show you where you are going to require cash (Current Liabilities).

You must understand Accrual versus Cash Accounting

As you may guess from this, there's two ways in which your accounts can be recorded; accrual accounting and cash accounting.

So why would you select accrual? Well, if you're only a 'one-man band' cash accounting is most likely all you'll need, but once you grow your accountant would most likely recommend accrual.

Why? It gives a better understanding of the healthiness of your business and is an important tool for its financial management. It shows the overall performance of your business during a period by matching income and expenses.

Irrespective of the cash flow, accrual accounting acknowledges income when a sale is made. In the same manner, it recognizes an expense when the expense is acquired.

Having said that, accrual accounting comes with some drawbacks. The primary disadvantage being the timing difference it produces between the recognition of income and expense transactions, and the true inflows and outflows of cash.

Cash accounting records the actual flow of cash through the company. It records income when cash is actually collected as a result of a sale and records expenses when a bill is paid. It's not concerned about matching income and expenses, but instead the actual inflows and outflows of cash.

The advantage is that it more closely mirrors cash flow.

There's one more distinction. Accrual accounting records a non-cash expense that decreases your profits - depreciation. Depreciation is an expense subtracted from your business income to mirror the annual cost of assets utilized in your business. Since the depreciation deduction is solely a "paper" expense, it requires no cash outflow.

Causes of Weak Cash Flow

As I talked about in the prior section, you can't pay bills without cash, regardless of how profitable your business, but there's an inherent difficulty in considering cash as being more significant than profit in the long run.

There's two issues here; working capital, and profitability.

Where does the cash go? Essentially, it's a blockage in working capital. The slower the working capital goes 'round, the more money you will need to operate your business.

There are three areas inside working capital. Each one can result in braking the process, slowing it down. The more sluggish the process the more cash it ties up. These three areas are referred to as WIP (Work in Progress), Stock (Inventory) and Outstanding Receivables.

It doesn't take a lot to clog up the process and get you in all forms of trouble financially.

For instance, WIP is just that. Something is being serviced, repaired, built, or manufactured. Until the job is finished it can't be sold, but while the job is in progress' it's accumulating costly hours and materials that have to be paid out.

Likewise, items in stock have to be paid for (your Creditors) however, you can't recover the money until they're sold.

To prevent cash flow problems, you need to turn things over frequently but if the cash flow is profitless, the slightest glitch or delay might find you facing a cash shortage and unable to pay the bills.

You must have a margin on the cash flowing through the business which you can hide away in your bank account. The larger that bank account the better position you are in withstanding that economic downturn.

This isn't to play down the importance of cash flow, but to reinforce the fact that the higher the margin, the better situation you will be in.

Also, the better you comprehend cash flow, the better you will be able to control your business.

The bottom line is the number one action you can take as a businessperson to improve your cash flow is to improve your profitability, not only your revenues.

But where do you begin?

CHAPTER 3

WHERE TO BEGIN?

In 2008 and 2009 nationwide economies were just starting to see some daylight ahead of the financial crisis. The next several chapters take a 20,000-foot view of what small business owners and managers could, and should, have been executing.

However, the advice is equally relevant now as when it was written. Additionally, it serves as a guide to the sections which follow.

AT CERTAIN TIMES IT IS FOOLISH TO ACT QUICKLY

The wise do everything in its proper time

A lot of us have been raised by parents who spent their youth in the Great Depression of the late 1920s and 1930s; and they heard all the tales of hard times, all of which were reinforced by many of the stories of difficult times in magazines and films. I was amazed to discover not everyone suffered. Many did, obviously, and the numbers were very significant in comparison to more typical times.

In the U.S. the entrepreneurs of some of the major cosmetics companies are often a quoted example of the wealth that was created in this period.

All of which is a roundabout way of leading up to a hypothetical financial crisis and what you as a small business owner or manager should do. It could be tempting to try to seem decisive by leaping straight in, cutting and slashing overhead and costs, but there might be some unintended outcomes from doing those things. There might be a better return on your hard work if they focused on those areas that they will have the greatest impact.

The initial thing is keeping your wits about you. Take a step back, take a deep breath and take a calm look at the circumstances.

Think matters through before jumping into the fray.

With a bit of thought and evaluation you'll gain a better result for your business. So where to begin? AFS Profit's rule is that there are five broad areas that you can work on improving the prospects for your business.

1. Sales
2. Prices and Margins
3. Cost of Sales
4. Overheads
5. Productivity

Sales

Are you putting your time and effort into selling into markets that won't be as profitable as others, or sales that take more time and energy to close? At times like these you need to focus your efforts on where you're going to obtain a real return. That raises the question of whether you know which sales are the most profitable, and which are the least profitable.

Prices

Are you currently charging the prices you could, or should? Many companies leave money on the table simply by not charging the prices they could, usually out of fear of losing sales. Have you researched where you can increase the value to maintain your margin? If you allow price to be the only factor in the pricing decision, you will be constantly confronted with continually decreasing margins as your company's competitors attempt to undercut you.

Cost of sales

It's the volume of Gross Profits that will determine your overall profitability, not the volume of your sales. Are you able to lower your cost of sales by improving purchasing? Does your Cost of Sales include all variable costs to ensure you recover them against the sale, rather than out of overhead, and therefore profits?

Overhead

Are you aware how much it costs you to remain open every day? Many overhead expenses have to be maintained at reasonable levels. Cutting them out completely could be detrimental to the business. However, that does not mean there aren't savings to be had. A great place to start could be those overhead expenses that you may not have requested quotes for a while, or not at all. Reducing the fixed costs will lower the quantity you have to sell (at a given Gross Margin) to break even. Everything above that is pure profit!

Productivity

Think about the working capital cycle and how effectively money is being used. Are you able to reduce the amount tied up in Debtors by not having them? Whenever possible get deposits on work, negotiate progress payments, and encourage clients to pay by credit card.

How much money have you tied up in inventory? Are you able to lower the amount of cash tied up in inventory by increasing stock turn and only stocking those items which turn over rapidly or are the minimum you need?

Opportunities for improvement in productivity could also lie in lessening errors and waste (are you measuring these?) and improving systems and processes.

In order to undertake the analysis that will determine the areas that will produce the greatest return will take some time, and require information which your company may not generate consistently but you'll make better, and more effective, decisions if you are in possession of the facts and data.

It's incredible how often having the facts available enables you to make effective decisions, a point that my 30 years of business experience has continually reinforced.

Getting the proper information may not be easy to obtain, but once you set up the techniques to have this flow automatically generated from your financial statements, you will have a much clearer understanding of your profits, or lack of profits. You'll be able to determine if you are remaining in markets which are less profitable than others. Sales data alone will not determine this.

You'll be aware of where the most probable cost savings are, and where cash can be freed up.

Executing everything in its proper time, with the data to support it, along with a little thought and analysis will go a long way to protect and improve your position. You'll literally create your own future.

CREATE YOUR FUTURE IN FIVE STEPS

Or perhaps the future is simply a place you are going?

There's no question that in trying times some people sharpen their wits and think more constructively. They need to if they're to survive. It probably accounts for the reason, as I referred to previously, many fortunes launched in the Great Depression of the 1920s and 30s. Comparable achievements have developed out of other and more recent economic downturns.

So, where will this leave you in challenging economic conditions? Australian writer and commentator Phillip Adams some time ago said "The future is not some place we are going but one we are creating. The paths to it are made, not found, and the activity of making them changes both the maker and the destination."

Or to put it a different way, you make your own luck. In making your own luck you are going to change yourself in regard to your own capabilities and skills, and your personal views of your future.

It's been interesting to watch a number of the small business owners I have known create their own future, grow their companies, perhaps beyond something they couldn't even contemplate, and grow themselves dramatically in the process.

The difficulties you will face as a small business owner and/or manager within the next year may be more significant than you are likely to have confronted so far during your lifetime. However, with these challenges come opportunities, opportunities to create your own future. The alternative is to be guided into someone else's future, and to settle for the inevitable consequences.

You don't need to accept these consequences. Nineteenth century British politician Benjamin Disraeli suggested "The secret of success is to be ready for opportunity when it comes" so what can you be doing to be ready for your opportunity to create your own future?

1. Focus on your key customers

Who are your key customers? They're those customers in market niches which provide the vast majority of your profits. Keep in mind the 80/20 rule. You'll earn 80% of your profits (and sales) from 20% of your customers.

Key customers will likely be buying from you with greater frequency, and in larger amounts, than other customers. They do so because you fulfill their needs; solve whatever business, personal, and/or emotional problems they have. They trust you and also believe they have developed a relationship with you.

During these times you'll want to work to preserve this relationship, nurture and protect them, and make certain that your competition doesn't manage to get their hooks in them.

There is of course a stipulation.

2. Research, research, research

What could bring you down, despite focusing on your company's key customers, is if their company or their market is adversely affected by economic circumstances. Many market sectors are probably going to be impacted one way or another by a poor economic climate sooner or later, but how significant is this probably going to be in the markets and customers you service?

Therefore, a little research is important. Regrettably most small businesses don't perform enough research. They depend on customers coming through the door. That may not be good enough.

Customers coming through the door might slow to a trickle if the economic circumstances negatively affect their company or marketplace.

There is a second part to the research you'll want to be undertaking, just as a safeguard. Yes, focus on, nurture, and protect your key customers, but in addition have Plan B.

Plan B is to have identified market segments that are being successful, or are likely to do just fine anyway, in addition also identify the prospective customers in these markets. Also, have a plan on how you are going to service them.

3. Understand your business

Truly understanding your business will allow you to both nurture your key customers, and to service Plan B customers.

The prior section recommended that doing everything in its proper time, with the data to support thought and analysis, will go a long way to safeguard and enhance your position during trying times.

You'll make much better and more effective decisions if you're in possession of, and understanding, relevant facts and data.

4. Ensure your marketing is effective

Ineffective marketing is a waste of one's time and money. There's only one justification for marketing, and that is to produce SALES. If your marketing is not driving sales, then it has cost you time and money and not generated a return. Yet another revenue leak!

Two crucial ingredients to make sure that your marketing is effective are the medium you employ, and the sales message it communicates.

Now is not the time for shotgun campaigns. The medium you work with needs to be razor targeted to your key customers, and not everyone in the population.

Be sure that your sales message addresses your ideal customers trouble and how your company's product or service will help them solve their problem. Ensure that your message also gets, and retains, your potential customer's interest, and then triggers them to take action.

5. Build your systems, procedures, and process's

All the great businesses I've seen have had good systems, procedures, and process's and *executed* them! Not merely scraps of paper to hand to a new employee declaring "this is how we do this", but correctly documented process's, well organized, and easily accessible.

The chances are that you've established sound process's, especially if you have been in business for several years. But equally probable are the chances you haven't documented them. Documenting your process's really does make a difference. It also makes sure that you make fewer mistakes which have to be paid for.

A journey of a thousand miles begins with the first step. These five steps can get you on the path to creating your own future and change both you and your destination in the process, but you have to *execute!*

But who does it start with?

CHAPTER 4

IT ALL BEGINS WITH THE CUSTOMER

The successful producer of a product or service sells it for more than it cost him to make it, that's his profit. However, the customer buys it only because it's more valuable to him than what he pays for it, that's his profit. No one can make a profit for long producing anything unless the consumer makes a profit using it.

Yes, it all begins with a customer. But do you actually know who your customer is. One thing is certain; you're not your customer.

Edward Demming, the initiator of Total Quality Management (TQM) and the Father of modern day management, said that the customer was the most important part of the production line.

Your focus on marketing should be on the marketplace, not the product - If marketing were supposed to focus on your product, it would be called "producting.". The marketplace is made up of people: customers and prospects.

JUST WHO IS YOUR CUSTOMER?

While the money is obviously important, it pays the bills and gives you your profits, business originates from customers. Without them all the financial KPI's aren't likely to tell us anything except there isn't any money.

Which leads to the significance of correctly identifying your customer. It is usually extremely expensive to go chasing after the incorrect customers, or to give the correct customers the wrong message; a genuine area for profit and loss.

In regard to your marketing and advertising, are you talking to yourself or your competitors or are you talking to your prospects and customers?

It's important to remember that you aren't your customer. The mindset that will make you successful is one where you constantly see your business through the eyes of your customer. The customer or prospect doesn't care about you, your business, or your product or service. All that matters to them is, What's in it for me?

Unless you're speaking with your customer, in language they will understand, you're wasting your time. And time is money. Rest assured, you are losing profits. Squandering your marketing time and money isn't just when you are talking to yourself or your competitor. It will also occur when you're speaking to the wrong customer, or when you choose the incorrect medium for your message. Even if you're speaking to the right customer but fail to give them compelling reasons for them to use your products or service, it will be wasteful.

Marketing legend Dan Kennedy suggested that it's infinitely simpler and always more profitable to work at increasing the purchasing of your completely satisfied customers compared to going out and adding new ones, which explains why *wise marketers make initial sales to obtain customers. Foolish marketers make initial sales to make a profit.*

What are the characteristics of the right customer and what do they want? I don't mean the demographics or even the psychographics of your company's customer. I mean their inclination to purchase. The wise Peter F. Drucker wrote, "The aim of marketing is to know and understand the customer so well the product or service fits them and sells itself."

You really have two tasks: to identify your target customer, and to discover what they really want? After all, they're not likely to buy unless they are able to see what's in it for them. And what's in it for them can't be a generality, it needs to be something specific to captivate their interest.

What's required is a customer profile, a profile specific enough to ensure that when you put out your promotional material that customer will say "They're talking to me!" And if he / she knows that you're talking to them, then they are more inclined to follow the promotional message to the end, and to make a purchasing decision.

HOW TO DEVELOP A CUSTOMER PROFILE

What exactly do you know about them?

The previous chapter examined customers and recognized that business starts with customers. Without having customers, we don't have a business. Who is your customer and what do you really know about him / her?

Customers buy due to self-interest, "what's in it for me?", occasionally referred to as WIIFM. To get their interest, your offer has to be targeted enough to their problems or conditions to attract their attention. Remember, they don't buy your product or service. They buy what your product or service does for them.

I recommended that one way to identify your customer would be to develop a profile of them; a profile adequately detailed to enable you to create a specific offer which will be of great interest to THEM and then they follow your message through to making a decision to purchase.

You can easily get drawn into what Gattari and Mooney call "silver bullet" marketing, which often entails costly advertising, graphics, and a new website and signage. This can be a way too common mistake that a lot of small businesses make. They're looking for the immediate solution to their marketing requirements and think (hope) that a single silver bullet is going to be it.

So frequently they believe that they need to promote to the fictional 'everyone' so that they don't miss a sale. However, by targeting everyone they are likely to get 'no-one'.

That's the whole idea of creating a profile of your ideal client. By creating a profile, you will find yourself speaking to a specific individual and addressing their issues, which means that you will be addressing WIFFM for them.

Is that important? Well, what makes an ideal client? Certainly it is somebody that buys more, considerably more, than the typical customer; someone to who you are going to sell more.

And that's why the profile you create is critical. It directs your attention and energy in the direction of those who find themselves more likely to buy from you, and also to keep on buying, and away from those who are less inclined to respond to your campaigns.

If you have an existing business that should provide you with a clue regarding how you develop a profile of your ideal customer. He / she will already be your customer.

Knowing some of the Key Performance Indicators relating to customers may help:
1. Average sales per customer
2. Average Gross Profit per customer
3. Customer Recent Purchase History
4. Customer Frequency

5. 80/20 customers

Start with number 5. It's almost certain that the ideal customer will be among the list of 20% of customers who constitute 80% of your company's sales. Can you identify those customers who purchase 'above the average' sales per customer and provide 'above the average' Gross Profit per customer?

Another qualification is going to be how frequently they purchase, and the time gaps between their purchases.

Develop a spreadsheet, list your top customers, and fill in the cells based on these questions. What did you find? There might be some customers who purchase infrequently but their purchases are high value and high Gross Profit when they do purchase. Others may make smaller purchases but do so considerably more often. Only you can determine who is 'ideal' in your eyes.

When you have a shortlist of potential ideal customers start looking for other differentiating features and characteristics. Are they a business or an individual, if it is a business, what kind of business, how far away are they located, what are they purchasing?

What else do you know about them? Personal things that could be additional determining factors in their buying behavior; age, gender, profession, education, etc. All these will vary from market to market so you have to find the characteristics that are important in your market.

Where do you get this information?

Well, much of this information will be in your management information system. Your financial accounts are going to have details of all sales and (hopefully) associated gross profits, date and value of purchases, etc.

The second source? It's the customers themselves. Asking them about their needs and wants and the difficulties they are looking to solve when buying from you, won't only help develop a useful profile, but it's also great for strengthening your customer relationships.

Then you define the profile by the greatest problem the ideal customer has.

That's important, because the customers you'll need more of will be the 20% of your total customers who make 80% of your sales, and not the 80% of customers who make 20% of the sales. They've got a reason for making those purchases.

But wait – there's more! You might have noticed a variety of groups of customers when you did your analysis. These different groups will be purchasing different products or services from you.

You can see it already, can't you? You will definitely need a variety of profiles for different customers with different wants and needs you can satisfy, sticking with the 80/20 rule of course.

Now you're prepared for some targeted promotion. No silver bullets, only a number of targeted bullets around which to build your marketing.

CHAPTER 5

AND NOW, MARKETING

Marketing is among those words that folks loosely toss around, typically without really understanding what it means for their company. Some consider marketing as promotion; others consider it selling (and you don't want to do that!). Many others consider it to be one's business identity, generally depicted as their brand. Every one of these are important.

Peter Drucker (The Practice of Management) stated "Marketing is the distinguishing unique function of the business. A business is set apart from all other human organizations by its marketing activities. Any organization that fulfils its purpose through marketing is a business, and any organization where marketing is absent, or incidental, is not a business, and shouldn't be run as such."

He also said "Because its purpose is to create a client, the business has two - and only two - functions. Marketing and innovation. Marketing and innovation produce results, all the rest are costs..."

As mentioned earlier, marketing should really focus on the marketplace - and the marketplace is composed of people: customers and prospects. You can get away without having marketing for some time but as time passes without marketing your business won't amount to much, and that's okay if that's all you want.

However, if you bought this book, then I believe you want more, and to acquire more you will need to master some primary marketing principles.

MASTERING CORE MARKETING PRINCIPLES

There are some who were trained in the 4 P's of Price, Product, Promotion, and Place as being the basis for a marketing plan. This has been, and remains, a very useful basis to prepare a marketing plan. However, I'd like to investigate another approach which you may find helpful.

I first discovered the approach below, when performing research for a presentation on marketing to a business group. I found it a useful way of rethinking the conventional way of developing a marketing plan.

They are "The 5 P's of Marketing" and I found they simply make more sense.

POSITIONING IS FIRST

This is about understanding exactly what your marketing and selling and who you're selling it to. Sounds straightforward, but many companies have a genuine problem with this one. It's about clearly identifying how you would like to be thought of in the marketplace. This is a crucial step since it will determine the rest of your marketing strategy.

You could have an excellent product or service, however, if you can't properly articulate why anyone would be considering what you have to offer, all the selling skills on the planet won't help you much.

Positioning revolves around a "Core Marketing Message" that clearly says whom you work with, exactly what problems you solve, what solutions your business provides, what benefits you are offering, what results you produce, what guarantee you provide, and what's unique and exclusive about your specific product or service.

Positioning is the foundation on which you will build the rest of marketing.

PACKAGING IS SECOND

Packaging is how you put your positioning strategy into words, both verbally and in the writing. Once you open your mouth to share with someone what you do, you're packaging yourself. Your business card, brochure, and website are physical, tangible methods you package yourself, largely through the written word.

Until your packaging is put together, you're going to find it difficult communicating to anyone about why they must use you. Packaging is the tangible side of Positioning. It's taking your Core Marketing Message and making it real.

Packaging the services you provide is about crystal clear communication. It has to broadcast directly why your products or services are of value, in addition to generating attention, interest, desire and action (AIDA) from your prospective clients.

PROMOTION IS THIRD

The objective of promotion is to acquire highly qualified prospective customers through the door, or on the phone. When you know what you're selling and it's in a form that folks can understand, you can begin spreading the word.

What works to promote your products or services? You'll find dozens, if not hundreds of ways for you to promote yourself, but ultimately the secret is to use the data and knowledge you possess, the same data and knowledge you sell to your clients, to market your enterprise. This is a key factor. Your knowledge and skill allow you to solve customer's problems. In the end, all sales are about resolving problems in one shape or another.

Promotion is focused on visibility and credibility. People love to do business with organizations and people who are familiar to them. Regardless of what promotional methods you utilize, you'll want to ask if you have adequate ongoing visibility to create that feeling of familiarity and trust. If you're invisible, nobody is thinking of you, not to mention calling you.

PERSUASION IS FOURTH

The job of persuasion is to convert prospects who've responded to your marketing into paying customers. Here's where sales or persuasion techniques and skills are crucial. If you can master the art of converting a large percentage of those that call or visit into paying customers, you'll possess a highly successful business.

Persuasion isn't about convincing people how fantastic your products or services are; that's more the job of packaging and promotion. Persuasion begins when people contact you in response to your marketing.

Persuasion is mastering the skill of listening and focusing on the wants, needs, and objectives of your customers. Then it's discovering creative ways to meet those wants, needs, and objectives, that are solving their problems in a way that's agreeable to both parties.

PERFORMANCE COMES LAST

But definitely not least. Not surprisingly, if you don't *execute*, meet customer's expectations, go the extra mile, and ultimately create "Raving Fans," you're not likely to have a lot of luck in growing your business. Its word-of-mouth marketing which finally determines most small businesses failure or success. So, your job is to deliver the goods and keep those referrals coming in.

Performance is a lot more than getting the job finished at an advanced level. It's about focusing on every single thing that impacts the customer experience.

Performance is about perception - the perception of the customer and their own expectations. Once you understand those perceptions and expectations and can also deliver what they really want, you've mastered performance.

As I mentioned previously, there are a variety of other P's in marketing! I might add Process, People, Presentation, and Pay plans but all that are important in marketing your business are usually included in these 5 P's.

BUILDING A 5P MARKETING PLAN

Building a marketing plan requires a strategy for each of the 5Ps in the previous chapter. To be able to do so requires you to be able to answer a number of questions under each element.

A 5 P marketing plan is a matter of developing a complete strategy for all the 5 Ps. One way to do this is to ask marketing questions for each of the Ps and then go to work in answering those questions. I've listed the key questions and the main things you need to do to market yourself below.

POSITIONING YOUR BUSINESS

What is the problem or problems your business is solving for your customers? They don't care about you, they only care about what you can do for them

What exactly is your business solution? That is, how does your product or service solve that particular problem, alleviate a pain or add value for the customer?

Who exactly are your targeted potential clients? Where are they; what industry; what size; what needs; what experience with your product or service and what buying process? You know by now that your market is not 'everyone'. What are the adjectives you'd use to describe your ideal clients - innovative, conservative, leading-edge?

What are the specific direct and indirect benefits your customers receive? What advantages, improvements or enhancements do your customers get as a result of working with you? What results can they expect?

What is your unique competitive advantage? That is, what differentiates you from your competitors? What do you do better, different, faster, cheaper, with higher quality or with a different spin? Can you be specific, not vague? This is always hard, but if you can't identify a key point of difference, you may be reduced to competing on price, and I'm sure that you don't want that.

What is your business identity? What are the qualities you want to be known for? Is it integrity and dependability or expertise and exclusiveness? You can't be everything to everybody. Next ask yourself what you are doing to live up to these qualities. The proof of the pudding... This ties back to 'branding' which I discuss later.

PACKAGING YOUR SERVICES

Do you have an attractive and appropriate Business Identity Package consisting of a logo on a business card, letterhead, and envelopes? This is the look for your business and needs to express your identity and positioning strategy. It is also reflected in the appearance of your business premises, appearance of staff, equipment, and vehicles.

Do you communicate the value of what you offer in everything you do? Do your prospective clients understand immediately what's in it for them if they use your services? Do you emphasize benefits and results over features and processes? Can you distil this down to a one, or two, page Executive Summary? Being able to do so is very important in preparing proposals, quotes, and tenders.

Do you have basic marketing materials (brochure or other printed material, website) for your business? These materials should include, but not necessarily be limited to: An overview of the problem that you have a solution for; an overview of your solution; a description of your Unique Competitive Advantage; a listing of your key customer benefits; a listing of your various services; testimonials from satisfied customers; a listing of customer or client companies; biographies of company principals; information on how to contact your company and how to do business with you; your address, phone, fax and email numbers.

Do you have a process of pricing your services and preparing proposals? Are you value-pricing, that is selling a solution, instead of your time? Are you sure to include objectives, value and measure of success in your proposals? Do you avoid "giving it all away" when you prepare a proposal? Do you know how to hold the line on your fees by subtracting value if they want to lower the price?

Have you put some attention on your personal package, your personal presentation? Whether you're a professional service business, do repairs and maintenance, etc., you are selling YOU and your expertise. You're the package. People make a dozen or more assumptions about you and your business in the first few seconds after meeting you in person or talking to you on the phone. Are you walking your talk?

PROMOTING YOUR SERVICES

Are you building relationships through authentic marketing activities? Are you doing everything possible to share information that will be valuable to your clients and prospects? Educating your clients is one of the most effective marketing tools you can use.

Do you have strategies in place for generating referrals? Are you providing a high level of customer service? Are you communicating clearly about your benefits and advantages? Are you asking for referrals when appropriate?

Do you stay as visible as possible to your clients, prospective customers, and associates? Do you belong to any networking organizations, volunteer or community groups? Do you get actively involved in these organizations? Do you have a website with all the information about your business posted so that people can learn more about what you do and how you can help them?

Do you do personal PR such as speaking and writing? Are you speaking at community groups, chambers of commerce and professional associations? Are you writing for community papers, newsletters, the trade journal for your industry, for web sites? Are you leveraging these speaking engagements and articles by inviting those on your list, getting reprints of articles, turning talks into articles and articles into talks?

Are you mailing or emailing to people on your customer list? This is an absolute must. Don't let people forget who you are and how you can help them. From six to twelve times a year are you sending clients and prospects a newsletter, or other type of keep-in-touch mailing? How else do you keep your business in the front of customer's minds so when they have a problem, your business is the first that comes to mind?

THE PERSUASION PROCESS

Do you have an elevator pitch or something similar? When someone asks, "what do you do?", do you have a concise and powerful solution statement that expresses what you do in a nutshell? Is what you say totally focused on what you can do for them? Do you always answer the question, "What's in it for me?"

Do you spend the majority of your time in a sales situation, on the phone or in person finding out about the needs of your prospect? Do you have a series of well-thought-out questions that help you learn about their situation, their problems, and the implications of not taking action?

Do you ask future questions of your prospects? That is, do you ask questions to determine not just what problems they want solved, but what they want things to be like once you've helped them? Do you dig in and determine exactly what objectives they need met in order to be satisfied?

Can you present what it is you do in a benefit-oriented presentation? Once you know the situation, problems, and objectives of your clients, can you outline a course of action that will solve those problems and meet those objectives? Can you put all of this into a concise proposal?

Do you wait for people to take action or do you move the action forward? Are you comfortable about recommending a course of action? Can you do this appropriately, without pressure or manipulation, outlining the advantages of moving forward with the project?

PERFORMANCE IN YOUR COMPANY

Are you proficient at communicating with customers in every stage of the process, starting with the sales process, through the proposal or quote, and into executing the work? Are you clear in regard to what you will do, when you will do it, and what outcomes they can expect? Do you structure things so there are minimal surprises?

Do you make promises you can keep? Are you conscious of your abilities and limitations and only make promises that you can achieve? Do you manage expectations so that you can always execute at a level above the promises you make? Your clients will judge you, not on what you promise but, on what you actually do.

Do you make requests of your clients so that they understand what you expect of them? Do you define the accountability of each person so that misunderstandings don't occur? When agreements are broken by your client, are you able to discuss it and get things back to normal right away?

Do you go one step further to develop "Raving Fans?" Are you continuously working to enhance your skills in every area of your business? Are you developing a network of resources that can help your customers in areas where you don't have the knowledge? Are you seen as the ultimate resource for your customers?

Are you clear regarding your purpose and vision for your organization? Do you have a statement of the vision and written goals that you are constantly moving towards? Do you do the things necessary to, not only make your customers successful but to, make your business successful, gratifying and fulfilling?

That might seem like a lot of questions, however if you can answer them you'll be able to produce a very practical marketing plan. Even trying to answer them should lead you to think deeply about your company, your market, and your offering.

It offers the opportunity for some considerable improvement.

What happens to your business if you don't perform some practical marketing?

You focus on the job at hand. Understand it properly to ensure you make a profit and then move on to the next job. That's all that's needed to build a business, isn't it? After all, there will always be a job at hand, and one to follow that. Life continues. Nothing much changes. Is this you?

I've known many companies like that. Just working away at their business, often doing it well, but not paying any attention to the outside world at all. And the funny thing is that it's not only really small companies that behave like this. Many larger ones do so as well.

Perhaps it is a coincidence, but companies such as these hardly ever seem to do any marketing, without recognizing the risk this places on the company. They rely almost entirely on word-of-mouth and repeat business to sustain them. There is nothing wrong with either of those: word-of mouth continues to be the most effective type of promotion. And repeat customers are the best customers to have. You make far more from repeat customers than you do from new clients, a fact that has been proven over and over again.

However, the idea of using either as a realistic marketing strategy is the last thing on their mind. Most likely this is because marketing reeks of selling. And selling is.........well, the picture that most likely comes to mind is that of a used car salesperson, or realtor. Both may be unfair pictures, but that's another issue.

However, the question that small business people ask is, "So what is the problem with their lack of strategy?" I would answer there are at least two problems.

The initial problem is one of insufficient control over the future path of your business. With no marketing strategy developed to achieve certain goals you have virtually no control over the future direction of your business. You're totally dependent on what comes through the door.

And what comes through the door may lead you down another path, which may conform at the time in terms of workload, but will be leading you down the wrong road. This happened to a client of mine. They found themselves with a totally different product and customer mix than the prior year. The really scary thing was this nearly caused them to make a decision to move from their field of expertise right into a larger, but very competitive, market where they had absolutely no competitive advantages whatsoever.

Without a competitive advantage they'd have been forced to be competitive on price, not value, thereby leaking revenues.

The second problem, an absence of practical marketing, is also a revenue leak, but a revenue leak in another form. Undoubtedly, taking whatever work comes through the door can result in your business doing jobs that you're not as expert in as others, work in which you might be less inclined to complete the job within the costs allocated. The feared cost overruns.

A cost overrun reduces your profit margin. In the event you don't think I'm right, try analyzing the past 15 jobs for how well you came in on actual costs versus budgeted costs. Chances are you will find the greatest variance will have occurred on the jobs outside your area of expertise.

Generally small business owners take these jobs as they come up because they're uncertain where the next job will be coming from. They'll view it as a form of security.

Wouldn't it be better to decrease the risk by making certain the jobs you get are taking your company where you would like it to go and also that these jobs are the jobs where you can add the maximum value through your expertise, and therefore profit accordingly?

You can accomplish this by adopting a simple and realistic marketing strategy to acquire referrals and repeat business without turning into a 'salesman'.

There's one more technique to learn, the one which leads to YES.

A NINE-STEP SALES PROCESS THAT LEADS TO SUCCESS

It seems some sales processes are universal, not learned by studying some 'expert' but by evaluating over time to uncover what performs and what doesn't. How many of you test your marketing or sales techniques to find out what works and what doesn't?

My wife and I were on a long-anticipated vacation. Rather than wandering around, into one tourist attraction or another without any idea of the story behind it, wanting to avoid the monotony of a busload of talkative tourists we chose individual guided tours of each destination.

There is another aspect to tours. Regardless if you are with the talkative tourists, or on a personal tour, at some point you will be guided to a shop where the merchandise will be showcased (with no obligation to buy of course) and 'sold' to you.

In some ways this isn't a bad thing. During our experience at least, you'll probably be taken to a reputable place with better quality products, instead of being left to the mercy of sidewalk vendors. Be aware of course that your guide will probably be paid a commission for anything you buy, at the very least 2 - 3% as one guide told us.

The sales lesson was in the way the sale is achieved, a nine-step process which leads to YES.

First comes education. The skill and expertise of the artisan is shown, working in the conventional way to produce the product. Authentic craftsmen from the towns where the work is done.

Secondly you are asked to appreciate how the expertise is employed and how such expertise is a dying art in this rapidly changing world (used to build up the scarcity effect).

Thirdly notice the assortment of finished goods that are available (more education, but also attempting to identify your point of interest).

At some point the Law of Reciprocity is presented into the process. This is when a sense of obligation is generated so that you will begin to feel at some point that you need to reciprocate by purchasing something, but something small of course. There's always a bit of reciprocity from the demonstration as well. At some stage a tea, coffee, or water is offered, no charge of course, so you "accept a little hospitality" building on the Law.

Then their USP (Unique Selling Proposition) is shown - why these goods are so distinctive from anything that you can purchase elsewhere - the fifth step.

Then the tipping point process is started, the sixth step. The first goods that are demonstrated are well within your price range and your interest starts engaging. Of course, you can afford the item.

Graduation - the seventh step. Having obtained your involvement, more goods are brought out, each one of higher quality and craftmanship, and a higher price tag of course. So, you pick up the product, hold it up to the light, take a step back and examine it.

You touch it, feel it, you can see it in your home. There's nothing like engaging the imagination, which of course is what every tourism brochure does with its beautiful photos - **can't you see yourself having that experience, the eighth step**.

At this point you are well beyond the moment of that low-priced item you initially considered, the one which took you past the tipping point. **The real question is no longer whether you are going to buy, but what you are going to buy - the ninth step**.

Yes, it worked on us, even while I admired the process. But why did it work?

As a process it works because it has been tested and improved upon over time, quite a long time. It mirrors the process that so many sales gurus will tell you to adhere to. However, they developed their expertise in an entirely different marketplace. It just happens to be a universal process that is effective.

And that's the point. Evaluate the process the next time a sales expert gives you a presentation. Now onto the role of Branding!

CHAPTER 6

THE ROLE OF BRANDING

A nd now for a completely new direction. A direction that always has implications for "revenue leaks".
In a previous chapter I discussed preparing for some targeted promotions by creating profiles for different customers with different requirements you can fulfill while still sticking to the 80/20 rule.

What are these customers expecting of you? The solution lies in what your brand represents for them.

HOW BRANDING CAN INCREASE YOUR PROFITS

Powerful brands make purchasing decisions easier!

Brands are amusing things. Some are immediately recognizable, such as the Golden Arches or Coke. You can picture them immediately, and not just the logo, but also something that you expect from the product; the taste, appearance, sensation, consistency, etc.

For these products or organizations, the brand is much more than the feel and look of the logo and its design. I recently read an article extolling the virtues of a logo. It's the first impression people have of your company and needs to last for many years. A logo can also be critical for its influence on the look and feel of other marketing materials.

That's all very well, but what the organization actually delivers is built into the brand, not the logo. Maybe we forget sometimes that with regards to our own businesses the logo is only one aspect of the brand.

Our greatest proof of brand success or failure is word of mouth.

Whenever people offer word-of-mouth recommendations to use your business, they do so because of the experience they've had with you. Here's the key: when they make a recommendation it's an emotional decision to do so. Making the recommendation is undoubtedly an emotional act.

The strength of branding originates from the emotional attachment it helps create for products and businesses. Emotion sells services and products, logic alone doesn't. Nine times out of ten, it's the heart which makes the purchase decision.

You have to think about what truly makes a brand, along with what enables it to permit people to take an emotional act such as recommending a product, service or business to someone else.

Take into consideration what they're saying to that other person. They're saying "you know me, you can trust what I tell you. Give it a try and you'll have the same experience or benefit I received!"

They are only able to say that if they believe your product, service or business will genuinely deliver that experience. All of which leads to the meaning of a brand.

The definition of a brand is "an identifiable entity which makes specific promises on value,".

In its most basic form, branding is nothing more or less than the promises of value that your product or service makes. These promises may be implied or expressly stated, but regardless, value of some kind is promised.

It's human nature to have an expectation of recurring performance. If you can control that expectation by reproducing that value, then the emotional attachment to you and/or your product or service will be reinforced by the other person's experience and multiplied. Failing to deliver the value as promised will let your client down, and with it their reputation.

Let's follow that reasoning through, moving from the person making a recommendation to the way you deal with the overall marketplace, and not simply the person.

You possess a brand, regardless of whether you formally create it, or otherwise. People deal with you and form perceptions about you and your business. They have expectations dependent on what you say, what your actions are, and what you promise.

Those perceptions and expectations with regards to you will be the heart and soul of your brand. It's not your logo or tag line. It's the value you provide, and the way you deliver it, that makes up your brand.

Every entity fundamentally has a brand. It's the constructing of a strong brand that you have to strive for.

Why? Because constructing a strong brand makes it much easier for customers to make purchasing decisions, to make the choice to use you and not your competitors.

Let's face it ... you don't even want to give your competitors an opportunity.

Powerful brands control buying decisions. What makes a strong brand is much more than the appearance and feeling of the logo. There's an instinctive understanding by your client that you'll provide them with something of value for selecting your products or services over your competitors.

They believe it's an implicit promise or pledge on the value you will deliver.

Certainly, a logo, a design, or a product package can't make this pledge or promise by itself.

If you asked your friends and customers what you represented..., what would be their responses? What would they say in regard to the value you deliver?

In the next chapter we'll take a look at how to build a strong brand.

CAN BRANDING MAKE YOU MORE MONEY?

You'll need more than advertising to accomplish this!

The previous chapter moved you from creating profiles of your ideal customers for targeting campaigns, to what those clients will expect from your business based on their expectations of your 'brand'.

I proposed that brands are definitely more than logos that they can form your expectations of the product or service; the taste, appearance, sensation, consistency, etc. What your business actually delivers is built into the brand, not the logo. The strength of branding originates from the emotional connection, it helps create products and companies.

You need to take into consideration what truly makes a brand, along with what enables it to allow customers to take an emotional action to recommend a product, service or business to someone else. As a result of such recommendations in the marketplace powerful brands control purchasing decisions. There is an instinctive understanding by your customer that you'll provide them with something of value for selecting your product or service above your competitors.

This chapter examines how to build powerful brands.

Powerful brands are designed from the inside out, out of your internal values, and out of your people, processes, and systems.

It's the way your team answers the phone, how straightforward your website is to navigate, what the subliminal promise your ads make, and the expectations they've created, the personality represented in your copywriting,... and if you're in retail, it's also the way your store appears and where you decide to have it. Brand will be the "experience" of doing business with you, in whichever way it occurs.

The fact is, brand is built and evolves each time a client or customer interacts with your business; they form a perception of both you and your business. That point of interaction is called "A Moment of Truth".

Branding is all about perception, and perceptions materialize from the way you deliver. To ensure an effective brand, you have to make sure it connects on an emotional level with consumers/clients.

People usually don't make rational decisions. They connect to a brand much the same way they attach to one another: first emotionally then logically. Likewise, buying decisions are made precisely the same way - first instinctively and impulsively after which those decisions are rationalized.

Emotions are the overlay for the motive. They're precisely what provides your customer's motives legs and produces action.

In order to manage your brand, you need to comprehend that your target market's perception can vary greatly from what you intend. To build the brand you have to make an effort to shape those perceptions and modify the branding strategy to make sure the market's perceptions become precisely what you want them to be.

In order to reach that goal, you'll need to know what the existing "experience of dealing with you" is from your customers eyes. As mentioned in the last chapter if you asked friends and clients what you stood for what might the responses be? What's the image you portray? Do you possess an on-going relationship with your customers?

John Forde, a noted copywriter, said "Is that why hype is dead? Is it why relationship marketing is the most powerful force online? Is it why so many marketers love to talk about "brand," not realizing that brands don't matter until a consistent relationship of quality has been established?"

I'd argue it is the "consistent relationship of quality" that is the brand. According to Glickman and Rubiner, "Treating prospective clients as a sucker born every minute may lead to quick sales, but it won't establish the enduring relationships which are the lifeblood of your company."

To know the nature of that relationship are only able to be found by asking your clients. It would be nice, but costly, to perform some research. However, you don't necessarily have to go that far. Create a few simple questions to ask them regarding their experience of dealing with you, and most importantly, take note of the answers. You have to record the answers so that you can analyze them and search for patterns. In my experience the patterns don't take very long to present themselves.

If those patterns indicate that there is a gap between your customer's perceptions of your brand, and the ones you desire, exactly what do you need to do to close that gap?

You don't need just "marketing" to be brand champions. Brand champions should come from every person in your business. Failing to deliver on a brand promise is brand suicide.

Remember, your brand is fundamentally a promise. It's a double-edged sword. Making a claim that is not supportable may get you a sale, but if you don't fulfill that claim, you will likely lose that customer - FOREVER!

I proposed earlier that strong brands are built from the inside out, out of your internal values, out of your people, processes, and systems. Closing the gap in customer's perceptions will demand progress in one or more of these. And it's a good chance that if you have failures in any one of them, there will be failures in others.

Therefore, you need good people, properly trained people who truly enjoy assisting your clients, supported by good systems and processes which enable them to deliver. Cheerful incompetence isn't enough to create on-going relationships. The following chapter completes this segment on branding along with some recommendations on branding strategy.

DO YOU REALLY NEED A BRANDING STRATEGY?

It can drive more revenue for you if you build the relationship the right way!

The previous section proposed that strong brands are designed from the inside out, out of your internal values, out of your people, processes and systems. Closing the gap in customer's perceptions will demand progress in one or even more of these. It's a reasonable chance that if you fail in any one of them, you will fail in others.

In other words, you need to have good people, properly trained people who truly like helping your customers, supported by good systems and processes which enable them to deliver. Cheerful incompetence isn't enough to develop on-going relationships.

How would you develop a branding strategy?

Let's begin with that consistent relationship of high quality I have been putting an emphasis on, and also the culture necessary to deliver it. After you have established that, then the method you use to deal with your clients will become as well-known as the products or services.

It will cut both ways. Staff members will both want to work with, and stay with, you because of the way they're treated. The outcome is a reciprocal effect where staff members create an encounter that blows customers away by showering them with excellent service.

As Kevin Freidberg, The Author of "Boom! Blowing the Doors off Business,", says: "Your brand is a promise of a pending experience as much for your employees as it is for your customers."

It says to your team: Come work with us and this is the type of experience you will have. These are the types of people that you will rub shoulders with. This is the type of work atmosphere you'll have.

Your brand says to your clients: Do business with us and this is the kind of encounter we will create for you personally. This is the type of quality you will experience with our services and products. The question then becomes: Will the encounter match the promise?

Brand strength is powered from strategic thinking, honesty, integrity, and commitment; commitment to developing the on-going relationship with all your customers. Once the brand is established, THEN advertising maintains it. Advertising doesn't establish your brand. If a small business thinks it could create a brand through advertising, then it should have very deep pockets.

If a brand is highly effective in making a bond with its target market and communicating its unique advantage, individuals will WANT to discuss it and word-of-mouth advertising will develop organically as well as the interest it's going to attract from the press and other media. That's the strength of a consistent relationship of high quality.

When that kind of differentiation is established in the market's thought process, advertising can then help to maintain and shape the brand, but it will never create it.

A great branding strategy deals with a number of key elements:

Its distinctive or has a point of distinction - The challenge then is locating your point of distinction and communicating that effectively to your target audience. Points of equality are those associations which are often shared by competitive brands. Clients view these associations as proof of authenticity within your category.

To put it differently, if you create what you consider being the quintessential point of distinction yet neglect to measure up to the "minimum product expectations" of your target market, your point of distinction won't be strong enough to sell your products or services.

Your brand should therefore consider and deal with your category's points of equality AND establish a point of distinction, i.e. your USP-unique selling proposition.

It's believable - Despite the fact that we already know that numerous brand choice selections have a strong emotional foundation, you have to make sure you offer adequate logical rationale to justify them. Remember, your brand is fundamentally a promise, a commitment.

It's relevant - It's not enough to notify your target market what you do; you must let them know how they will benefit by selecting your brand. From a marketing perspective, it is essential to ask, "Does my 'brand promise' really make a difference to my customers?"

"Is this the most inspiring way to present my brand?"

Whatever you decide to do, you have to remember this: Brands that flourish mirror their core culture and exclusive character, resolve relevant needs and deliver a consistent experience for their customers, and for their team.

The relationship is really what gets your messages opened. The relationship is really what gets the messages read, and also the customer through the door. The relationship is what makes way for the sale because of the trust that has been established. You can't simply build your "brand" image through strokes of cleverness and advertising slogans by themselves.

The best way to earn any type of noble brand position, in email or anywhere else, is by way of the quality of the product itself, and also the service that supports it.

That can only come from the inside out, through your internal values, through your people, processes, and systems.

That will also impact the price you can charge, and the perceived value you deliver.

CHAPTER 7

PRICING AND VALUE

There are plenty of words that modern society has placed taboos around. Every society has words and phrases that are inappropriate for whatever reason.

In business there's one word which makes most business owners so uneasy they often don't feel like discussing it, even when pressed. And it's not a four-letter word either. It's PRICE. Specifically, what their prices are and ways in which they establish them.

Pricing is one of the more important strategic judgements you make as a small business owner and/or manager. It's also among the least understood.

Prices are where all your marketing investment meets the moment of truth between your company (brand/product/service) and the client, the final results of which you determine in your financial statements.

However, four factors come into play.

The first factor is the fact that businesses constantly charge less than they can for new offerings, or worse, for most offerings. It's a terrible practice.

The second factor to be contended with is Marketing identifies price as one of the four key Ps in the marketing mix but there's minor linking of the marketing elements of price to the financial side of the company in regard to decision-making.

Should you have a poor outcome for the year, your accountant is as prone to say, "Raise your prices" without any thought of the impact of this on your position in the marketplace.

The third factor to take into account is fear, your fear, fear of losing your clients if you increase your prices. Is this you? It's a disorder that impacts most small businesses. It is a bad mistake to operate out of fear. And all the time costs are unnoticeably rising.

On to the fourth factor. How much time do you invest in considering your pricing strategy including how you set your prices? The majority of small business owners and managers invest less time considering their pricing strategy and the way they set prices then they do considering whether or not they should sponsor their children's sporting team. Yet it's a complicated task.

Price is really not the problem. Instead it's the lack of knowledge of different pricing strategies that confuses owners and managers. Additionally, the lack of knowledge leads to ineffective pricing strategies, or even the wrong pricing strategies. Poor management of pricing diminishes your profitability and ultimately places your company at risk.

ARE YOU CURRENTLY GETTING VALUE FROM YOUR PRICING?

How well you set your prices will be the issue here.

Your prices are one of the most direct ways you will be able to communicate value to your clients. Equally important is the prices you set have the most direct influence on your bottom-line effectiveness.

A quote in an article caught my eye because it dealt with a concern that is basic to your profitability. It related to how you price your product or service.

The quote was "The customer's assessment of value may be much more than the cost of the parts."

It brought to mind a problem a smaller client of mine was having. Among other activities Sam repairs components for aircraft. Aircraft components have to be repaired to a very high standard. After all you don't want to be flying in an airplane where price was more important than quality.

The quality is normally that components are as good as new. A new part of one specific component sells for approximately $8,000. And Sam, after calculating labor and materials, charges a little over $2,000.

At $2,000 do you feel he has some room to negotiate, that he could be leaving some profit up for grabs?

It's a pretty tricky matter, really. Aside from the bottom-line, it may also impact how your products or services are thought of. In the event you set your prices too low you may well be perceived as a commodity, leaving price as your main marketing tool. However, in the event you set your prices too high you take the risk of being priced out of your market.

There are also strategic as well as tactical issues. For example, you might not want to be viewed as a low-cost business, a strategic decision, but you may want to conduct a short-term promotion based around low prices. The risk is that in the event you keep that up for a long time you might alter the customer's perceptions of your overall price position.

Have you been setting your prices for profits, or for sales?

So how do you establish your prices? There's a couple of possibilities. Obviously, a lot will depend on the nature of the items you're selling. The more of a commodity it is, meaning there is little variation in quality or functions in the market, the more likely many people will choose to defect and buy, on price.

A second possibility is that you have to know your marketplace and how it thinks and responds.

Any marketing book will provide you with a whole range of common pricing policies. Policies such as:

Penetration Pricing - This is a strategy of lowering prices to increase sales volume as quickly as possible. It is dependent upon repeat business for continuing high sales quantity at a small profit. But be mindful of the effect on client's future expectations.

Cost-Plus Pricing - Pricing based on the cost of the product or service in addition to a minimum mark-up which you consider required to cover your costs and targeted profit. This strategy does not pay attention to the demand for the product or service or your competition. However, used properly it can be the foundation of achieving a targeted Return on Investment (ROI).

Bundling - Packaging a group of products together and selling them at a price below what the client would pay if he or she bought them separately. It may decrease your overall gross profit margin but improve the volume of gross profits, simply because you sell more than you would have.

Distress Pricing - Discounting is used to get rid of a discontinued or sluggish selling line. It's also useful for Close Out or Clearance Sales. Competition and / or demand has only minimal effect. It can result in customers' distrust of sale prices because some businesses have continuous sales.

Going Rate Pricing - Matching your competition for similar services or products, for example trades people and quite a few other personal services employing an hourly rate. To be successful, the overall marketing blend must attempt to add other advantages, e.g. service or convenience. A great number of small businesses pick the first part, matching the competition, but not the second.

Loss Leader Price - Selecting a few, "in demand" items which customers will recognize as good deals and utilize them to entice people to the business. Frequently used by retailers and made available in catalogs and promotions.

Every Day Low Price - another popular approach, a strategy of regularly offering a reduced price, but not the lowest.

Skim pricing - a premium pricing strategy of establishing high price margins within an innovative or low-competition market

Confusing isn't it? But in numerous ways practically all of these strategies miss the point. The following chapter examines what that point might be, and talks about an alternative approach.

I also give an example where I just got it completely wrong and messed up what should have been a profitable job.

An alternative approach to pricing

The 1st chapter in this segment looked at the issues of reconciling long-term objectives with short term campaigns. In the 2nd we looked at several of the traditional pricing strategies and concluded by suggesting these particular conventional strategies missed the point.

And the point is?

One of the differentiating features of the list above is the fact that not one of the strategies discuss value, that is, value in the client's eyes.

Whenever you bring value into the formula, it eliminates the cost side of the formula. This isn't to say that you ought to ignore costs. You need to know what your costs are. In fact, the price set also needs to deliver value to you in the form of profits.

What I'm suggesting is that by providing value to the client into consideration you will improve your profitability, often significantly.

However, it does mean you need to introduce value into your conversation with the client to move them from a 'comparison to the competition' mindset.

Let me provide you with an example of where I essentially messed up by not properly introducing value into the discussion.

A gentleman came to me with a proposal in which he needed some marketing assistance. It was a brand-new business, but greatly linked to an existing business he had. Consequently, he knew his business, and its marketplace. He'd done his profit-and-loss projections that were pretty good. They showed a profit of $80,000 at the conclusion of the first year and growing thereafter. Then he asked me for an estimation of what I would charge to create the marketing material.

I could create the marketing material, but it was in my response to his question that I came undone. It didn't take very long to calculate the time I would have to put into the work, which was probably a couple of days, apply my daily rate, and therefore I had a dollar amount. So I did that and let him know what it was.

He nearly fell off his chair, looked insulted, and then walked out.

But what would his response have been if I had asked him what he'd be ready to pay to earn $180,000 in the first year. I bet it would have been a much greater dollar amount than I had proposed, possibly around three times as much.

Had I introduced the value to him I would've gotten the sale and earned considerably more profit. Lesson learned.

How do you introduce value into the conversation? Here are 3 suggestions:

1. What amount will she/he earn from your product or service? Just like my potential, and lost, customer above, if he/she evaluates her purchasing decision in terms of the profit she would earn it would leave her with a different outlook.

2. "A stitch in time saves nine." Could your offer lessen the customer's costs, or save him / her time? Cost savings, whether it be time or materials, go directly to the bottom-line. If the client can visualize significant or on-going cost savings, they'll view the price in those terms, i.e. the value to them, and not the cost to them.

3. Will there be an emotional return to the client? Many sales today are made based on emotion rather than logic. Think of luxury cars, a stress reliever, plastic surgery, social activities, anniversaries, rewards. Emotion is tougher to place a figure on, but don't underestimate its value.

Why don't you get a cup of coffee and take some time to sit down and think about whether there is value in your pricing? If at the end of that cup of coffee you're unsure, then it's time to get some outside advice.

PRICE IS WHAT YOU PAY, BUT VALUE IS WHAT YOU GET

These types of issues resulted in a vigorous discussion at a seminar I performed, with accountants on one side of the room, and small business owners on the other.

The discussion focused on whether it was ethical and moral to earn large profit margins on a service or product if the client is willing to pay the price. A case in point is the example I gave in the first part of this section.

You'll recall a gentleman called Sam who repairs aircraft components to good as new condition. New components cost $8,000. Bill could repair the component and was charging $2,000, therefore leaving a lot of money on the table.

The question is, should he be charging more? He could, but should he? It was this basic principle that fueled the energy level of the discussion at the seminar.

There's a couple of issues here.

First, does the client have any idea of your costs, and should he/she? Typically, he/she is not likely to, and I doubt that you're very likely to tell her even if he/she were to ask.

Second there is the dilemma of whether there's such a thing as a 'reasonable' profit? What's reasonable in one situation may not be in another. And what are reasonable costs? Take Sam as an example. He is repairing aircraft components, and as I mentioned earlier, you wouldn't want to be flying in airplane where the basis of the decision where to have repairs done was price, not quality.

To determine Sam's price, he's most likely charging his time at say $75 per hour for repairing an airplane component. How does that compare to a partner in an accounting firm who might be charging $350 or more per hour? In under the circumstances, which is the more reasonable?

Surely the concept that the price you charge for your services and products should be primarily based, not on what it costs you to provide them, but on the value it provides to the client. They don't know your costs and, let's face the facts, they base their willingness to buy on an evaluation of the benefits it provides them compared to the price they pay. That is the value they perceive. Remember, price is what you pay, value is what you get.

And as a result, that means you need to have an understanding of how your clients perceive value; of what is important to them, of the difficulties they are looking to overcome by buying your products or services.

That's a totally new subject, and one that'll be addressed in another section. In regard to the vigorous discussion, what would be your thoughts?

CHAPTER 8

HOW TO BALANCE THE VALUE FORMULA

Pricing is a complicated issue, but so is value. How a customer perceives value, and its frequently intuitively, has to be understood if you're to balance the value formula.

There's two foundations to having an effective pricing strategy and they're both based upon knowledge: knowledge of your costs, and knowledge of your marketplace. Your price should be a market price, not a cost price. And that's where the value enters in.

What's that value really worth to the client, because that's what they're prepared to pay? The client doesn't know your costs. It's the value you add, the outcomes you deliver that the client is paying for.

Your client isn't buying your product or service based on what it costs you. He or she is buying based on the value it will provide to them. Will it save them money? Will it overcome an issue, repair something? Will it relieve the suffering? Will it allow them to do something faster, or easier? There's value in that.

Knowing your marketplace and the problems your product or service truly solves for your client, and the value it delivers, is crucial in having an effective pricing strategy. And if you can't provide that value at a cost that results in you making a profit, then you need to ask yourself whether you should be in that marketplace.

The only constant in life is change. An old saying, and it's true. Extraordinary changes in the marketplace can suddenly put your business in peril. Gradual changes in the marketplace can cause it to trickle away.

Let's start with the clients; the people without whom you don't have a company. They may not have changed as a target market however their expectations may have changed. Their inclination to purchase may have changed. Their particular buying patterns, and frequency of purchase may have altered, as well as the average value of their purchases.

Houston, we have a problem. So perhaps the symptom of a problem causing a revenue leak in your company is that there haven't been any clear enhancements in the customer offerings over time to satisfy what the customer now perceives as value.

Balance the value and improve your sales as well as your profits

Have you noticed the number of products and services that come in a variety of combinations, and in some cases a staggering variety?

Have you noticed that when Microsoft announces a new system such as Windows 10, it offers a number of different versions. You can get the Home Basic version, Home Premium, Business and Ultimate.

Auto manufacturers do the same thing. There's a basic model, to the XXX version that has a spoiler on the trunk large enough to land a helicopter!

Every version has an even greater number of features which considerably improve the offer and does so at an increased price. Occasionally the price variation can be quite substantial.

What are these companies doing and can you use the same strategy?

This strategy is all about creating an offering by way of different value packages focusing on different segments in the marketplace, thereby increasing sales. Great businesses do this by balancing the value formula, and there's no reason why you shouldn't do the same thing for your marketplace.

The secret to a value package is the sum a prospective customer pays, usually informally in their mind, but sometimes formally on paper. That sum is a calculation of the 'benefits' of the product or service minus its price', to come up with the sum, the 'value' to the customer.

So what do these terms mean?

Benefits

You'll be familiar with the need to focus on benefits rather than features when promoting your own products and services. Features are about the product while benefits are about what those features do for the client. Or another way to look at it is, features are the cause, and benefits are the effect of using your product or service. It's challenging for your prospect to perform a value assessment based solely upon descriptions of the features. They can understand and make judgements about what the product does for them when you give them the benefits.

But there's more to benefits than simple cause and effect'. There are at least two levels of benefits. Direct benefits are what people generally discuss. You go on a diet, and if you maintain discipline, you drop some weight. Cause and effect.

Let's take this a step further. Shedding weight is the direct benefit, but what's the resulting effect of having done this? Now that's where things get fascinating, because the indirect benefits can take several paths. You may:

· just feel great about yourself again, which is not a bad circumstance to be in
· have more energy, more pep in your step
· take up an activity again
· get work completed quickly and as an outcome, be able to spend more time with your loved ones
· be more appealing to your partner
· etc.

Have you detected that all these indirect benefits have to do with how you feel rather than something strictly measurable like the weight you've lost? Because they're about how you will feel, you have a tendency to evaluate them in emotional terms.

So many advertisements try to tap into our emotions. They ask us to place ourselves in the situation being presented. Very cunning, because many people make choices for emotional reasons, even though they justify them in more logical terms (I've lost 20 pounds!).

The benefit portion of the value formula is not as simple, however you need to understand it to 'balance the formula' when presenting an offer to your prospects.

And now on to price!

Price is the amount your client pays for your product or service, but there's a lot more to it than that. Price is more than the list price. It also includes warranties, the level of service they receive, the anticipated life of the product, lifetime costs, ease of access, speed of delivery, and a whole range of additional factors that your customer may take into account.

The more complex your product or service the greater these factors will enter into the value formula, and if ineffectively managed, they'll create doubt. For this reason, if you can clearly specify these components in your offer, you'll decrease the uncertainty in the clients' mind, and permit them to focus on the benefit part of the formula.

And also, if you base your prices solely on the costs to you, essentially you'll have very little control over the value formula. If the value you provide clients is clearly outlined this will give you an advantage over your competitors, and you can then charge according to the value you provide.

Ineffective management of price confuses clients, turns them away from your benefits, decreases your profitability, and ultimately puts your business in danger.

So, the value is:

Value occurs because the indirect and direct benefits your product or service provides solves a problem for your client for a price they're willing to pay in order to gain those benefits.

If it's too high a price, then your benefits won't be seen to provide value, and the client won't purchase, or at least, they won't purchase from you. Instead they may very well go to a competitor who provides an excellent value as perceived by the customer.

The better the benefits with regards to the problem they solve for the client, the more the client will likely be willing to pay to acquire those benefits.

Too low a price may offer increased value to the client, but at the expense of your profits.

The problem in getting the balance right is that frequently the assessment the client makes may very well be carried out in their mind. It's a perceived value, and each client will form their particular perceptions.

And now, back to that variety of offers.

You can see why Microsoft, auto companies and others developed a variety of offers building on a base service or product. Their different target markets will be looking for different solutions for the problem they're looking to solve. In regard to auto companies, what is one person's basic transportation is another's personal statement. So the auto companies seek to provide a range of solutions' by providing a range of value formulas.

We should conveniently group the most typical of these needs into market segments. Each segment will possess a different value formula to be balanced through the benefits they look for and the price they're willing to pay.

The next section examines how to build on the perceived benefits in order to tilt the balance in your direction and improve both your sales and your profitability.

TILTING THE VALUE BALANCE IN YOUR FAVOR

How to build perceived benefits into the value formula

The previous section looked at how organizations were able to use the same basic product or service and by supplying different value formulas, make various offers to different market segments.

The value formula is the calculation any buyer does, usually in his / her head, to evaluate the benefits your product or service provides versus the price. You saw that benefits are not a simple listing of features. They're what those features of your product or service do for the buyer, both directly and indirectly. Indirect benefits are usually about how the customer feels, so they often evaluate them in emotional terms.

Even though most people make decisions for emotional reasons, they justify them in logical terms.

You also saw that price is significantly more than list price; it consists of the level of service, guarantees, lifetime costs and a whole host of factors. The more complicated your product or service the more these factors will come into play in the formula.

I also suggested that if you base your prices solely on the costs you incur, and not on the value to the client, then you'll have little control of the value formula, you'll diminish your profitability, and ultimately put your company at risk.

Each market segment you support will possess a different value formula, even for the same basic product or service. In this section we look at how to build on the perceived benefits to tilt the balance to your advantage in the various segments you service.

So where will the value originate from, and what methods can you use to build on the perceived benefits? It shouldn't surprise you that those benefits will relate more to the emotional than the logical, especially as the cost increases.

If the service or product is basic, for example transportation, the direct benefits are essential. The vehicle gets the owner from point A to point B relatively safely and in reasonable comfort. It's when the buyer has additional expectations, beyond the standard, that the other factors come into play. That leads to the need to add indirect benefits in your offering. There's more value in the indirect benefit compared to the direct benefit.

Whenever you add to the indirect benefits you're offering, you'll be able to increase the price as a result of the value you're adding. You can use those additional indirect benefits to position your product or service in different segments than those serviced by the base product.

What are several of the ways in which indirect benefits may be used? Here are 5 which lay the foundation for most indirect benefits.

Relationship - people are typically tribal; they would like to be part of a community, a part of everything that is happening within their industry, in order to feel they belong.

At a low level of a relationship businesses offer loyalty programs. Loyalty programs are more than just a relationship, they usually offer a financial benefit such as discounts or "buy 4 and get 1 free", they also provide the illusion that you are part of a club.

Moving up the ladder, memberships offer exclusive and restricted offers, newsletters, and often access to special amenities. The more special benefits offered, the more you'll feel especially privileged, a 'relationship' with an exclusive group.

One retail business owner offers clients who purchase above a certain dollar amount the opportunity to enroll in a VIP Club, free of charge. Club members receive early notice and access to all sales and specials.

Can you develop a feeling among your customers that they are special and in a relationship?

Getting free items or upgrades or a bargain - adding additional features to a service or product can be employed to lift the product or service into a different segment. Cars are a good way to demonstrate the principle. Auto makers add more powerful engines, spoilers, power equipment, and other items to create a sportier model, or perhaps a package of additional features to produce a luxury model.

As a small business owner or manager, you're capable of the same thing by providing an enhanced warranty or guarantee, or a 24-hour support package. As another example a car sales person could give gift when the customer is picking up their new car. You can bet that the purchase of that car will be remembered and commented on which equals good word-of-mouth.

Additional significant features provide additional benefits thereby allowing you to charge a higher price. In fact, the prospect will expect to pay more. The new selling price is part of the different segment.

So where will the "free" or "bargain" come into play? Well, consumers are always searching for something free, or getting something at a bargain.

Adding a bonus in the form of additional features at a price below the apparent value of the add-ons will likely be viewed as creating additional value, particularly if the offer is for a very limited time. Or you could offer the benefit of a free 3-month trial.

The "bargain" helps move the prospect into the different segment.

Simple solutions to complicated problems - Usually people are searching out the simplest solution to complicated problems. If you can provide a step-by-step solution to a complex problem it will enable the customer to solve their problem easily, with minimal effort on their part. Weight loss programs will often be sold like this.

Selling a dream, making that dream become a reality - Presenting your product or service in an aspiring way. This elevates your service or product beyond the normal reasons for buying. Can your offer tap into their fantasy rather than their real life? Many people don't believe they'll achieve their aspirations. Holding out hope that they'll do so enables the client to connect with their dreams.

Price doesn't matter in these scenarios. When they're achieving that dream, price doesn't matter any longer. Aspirations have a tendency to be very powerful motivators.

Of course, you don't need to put things in magnanimous terms. Pictures of the customer enjoying a vacation, having a meal, or simply doing something enjoyable can achieve the desired effect. Testimonials may also be used to accomplish the same thing.

Fear of loss – Fear can be utilized when the prospect needs, or merely wants, what is being offered. Marketing your product or service as being in short supply, (limited quantities available) or for a limited time, suggest that unless they take action now they might lose out. Scarcity marketing is utilized to get prospects to take action.

Do you see that each one of these motivators are emotional motivators, and each one individually, or better still, used collectively, may influence the value formula a prospect makes, tilting the balance to your advantage?

And by varying the mix of them, or using various benefits to differentiate the product or service, you can

target your basic product or service into different market sectors, meeting different needs and expectations.

CHAPTER 9

DO YOU REALLY KNOW YOUR COSTS?

GRRRRR costs! Cost was forced to rear its ugly head at some phase. If it wasn't so serious it might be funny; the number of times clients tell me that they don't actually know their costs. They are fully aware of their sales prices, and exactly how much money they've got in the bank, however they don't know the real costs of the services or products they're providing.

If the truth be known, they didn't appear to have considered the issue at all.

It's similar to the old children's game of "Pin the Tail on the Donkey". They rarely get it right, and neither will you if you don't know your real costs and allocate them correctly. That is not to say that your prices should be based on your costs but that's another subject addressed in earlier sections.

HOW YOU CAN MAKE PINNING THE TAIL ON THE DONKEY MORE ACCURATE

It's much easier when you're not blindfolded

If you don't know your costs I'll guarantee that you could perform better, and that you're leaking revenues without knowing it.

What do I mean by that? If you don't know your costs, then you don't know your profit margin. And if you don't know your profit margin, then you don't know how much profit you could, or should, be making.

Which leads to the conclusion that achieving your target profit is actually like that blindfolded child who is able to pin the tail on the donkey in roughly the right place. It is a purely accidental occurrence over which they had no control.

Removing the blindfold is a simple matter. You just need to understand where your costs are incurred and allocate them accordingly. Then you'll know your actual profit margins and have pinned the tail on the donkey.

The problem usually occurs in one of two areas:

1. Improperly allocating costs to overhead instead of cost of sales; and
2. Not knowing your actual complete cost of labor.

Let's take a look at some examples of the first:

Failure to include costs which are directly attributable to a job or project can result in loss of profits.

1. A marketplace research project may require a lot of telephone work. Telephone costs are usually considered part of overhead but if they're disproportionately accrued against a project, then allowance should be made in the pricing.

2. Freight, either associated with incoming products and materials, or for delivery, is often buried in overhead. However, it's usually a variable cost directly related to Cost of Sales. This is easy to see if you're bringing in materials or parts for a specific job, but even if you are bringing in, for instance, steel plate for inventory, it's a variable cost. You wouldn't be restocking if the jobs weren't there. If the steel plate is really a cost of sale, so is the cost of the shipping to bring it in. The same can be applied in delivering the completed job to a client even if it's part of a delivery. The costs are attributable to the job.

3. Replacement tools - quite a few small hand tools are worn out throughout the year, with the rate of usage being directly related to the amount of work being performed. Therefore, they are a variable cost.

4. Shop misc. supplies should be treated similarly.

If such costs are not attributed to the Cost of Sales either directly or through calculation of the shop charge out rate since they become overhead and not included in the sale price. And as they aren't being recovered directly from the sale, they become an additional overhead cost which have to be subtracted from your Gross Profit.

While a number of items might seem to be relatively small, collectively they could add up to be substantial costs. And that's just what they are, costs. The important factor to consider is that if such costs are not recovered against the sale which incurs them, they come straight off your net profit.

As a cost they may seem small, but as a percentage of net profit they can be significant.

I'd add one other aspect to this. As a small business owner or manager, you need to differentiate between your income, the business pays you for your skill and experience, and the profit the business returns to you for the risk of investing in the company.

Your salary is not profit. It's the price of doing business. The profit your company should earn, after allowing for all salaries, should be equal to what you could earn by investing your money in a low risk investment.

The majority of you will make the distinction however some do not. Those that don't are truly just using their company to buy themselves a job.

Overall, you can see why people have been concerned. They aren't pinning the tail on the donkey because they can't see the donkey. They are operating their business blindfolded.

ARE YOU STUMBLING IN THE DARK WITH YOUR ACTUAL COST OF LABOR?

Is it time to put a little light on the subject?

The last section dealt with the problems for profitability brought on by improperly allocating costs to overhead versus cost of sales. The root issue for you is when you don't know your cost of sales then you'll have no control of your profits.

Just like the blindfolded child business owners are trying to pin tail on the donkey with no knowledge of which end is which.

The 2nd issue on this topic covered the dilemma of not being aware of your actual full cost of labor.

To determine your actual cost of labor, you have to calculate not only the direct cost of labor, but also the percentage of overhead each chargeable hour will have to recover before you could generate a profit. This is commonly known as a "Full Recovery Rate".

The initial step is to calculate the available hours per person per year. Please be aware the numbers listed here are examples only. You'll need to use your own numbers.

Total Weeks - 52
Vacation (weeks) - 4
Sick leave (weeks) - 2
Public Holidays (10 days) - 2
Available Weeks Remaining - 44

Hours worked per day - 8
Days worked per week - 5
Total Hours/per person/per year - 1760
Efficiency factor - 80%
Available hours - 1408

Please note the efficiency factor. In fact, we don't get 100% utilization out of our team. They're not robots, punching in and going right to work, efficiently going from one job to another with no break. In addition, for hourly workers an allowance has to be made for unapplied time Hours per Day - Traveling between Jobs, Callbacks, Paperwork, etc.

From an operations viewpoint this efficiency factor is a lot lower. As a manager you need to perform administrative work, marketing and advertising, possibly quoting and other functions that are nonproductive from a billable standpoint.

Direct cost of labor - The 2nd requirement is to calculate your direct hourly labor costs, taking into consideration that you have to pay your employees while they're on leave, health care costs, as well as any other costs directly related to employees that might be applicable to your situation. (Note the figures used here are examples - insert your own costs and categories.)

Annual Salary - $ 45,000.00
Bonus @ 9% - $ 4,050.00
Health Insurance @ 3.50% - $ 1,575.00
Total Cost - $ 50,625.00
Available hours - 1400
Hourly rate - $ 36.16

Therefore, in this example, a person may be costing you $36 per hour prior to any contribution to overhead or profits.

Spreading the fixed cost of operations - a full recovery man hour rate spreads out the fixed costs of operating the company across the expected available hours for the year. For the purpose of this calculation I incorporate those variable costs referred to above including replacement tools, consumables, and also freight if these have not been individually identified in the cost of sales.

The subsequent steps would apply.

1. How much is it likely to cost you to open the doors every day?

What are the common overhead expenses you're likely to incur given your present or anticipated business activity?

Include all fixed expenses, an income for yourself, all of your staff costs, phone charges, stationary, etc.

However, don't include the cost of goods you purchase to complete a particular project.

2. How much profit would you like to make?

A good beginning would be to look at the capital you have invested in the company and calculate a commercial return on your investment. Have you considered your intellectual capital? What's that really worth and what return would you like on that? You also need to take into account the risk factor.

3. How much time do you have available?

Now multiply the hours per employee determined above by the number of employees you have.

(Please refer to the example calculation below.)

Example Calculation

Direct Cost per Employee - $36.16

Overhead - Fixed Costs

Advertising & Marketing Expenses - $17,011

Bank & Government Costs, interest - $46,470

Donations/Sponsorships:

Utilities Expense - $2,697

Insurance Expenses - $6,182

Vehicle Expense (Gas, Maintenance, etc.) - $32,778

Printing, Postage & Stationery - $1,000

Safety Equipment Expenses - $3,000

Office Rent / Lease Expenses - $15,000

Subscriptions, Licenses & Training - $1,500

Telephone Expenses - $6,348

Salaries/Wages for Unapplied Time: $52,777

Staff - $0

Management Fees / Expenses - $0

Depreciation of Vehicles, Plant & Equipment - $3,000

Misc. - $2,000

Total Overheads - $19,4327

Number of employees whose labor is billable (Full time equivalent) - 2.5

Billable hours per employee - 1,400

Total Billable hours - 3,500

Overhead per Billable hour - $55.52

Bill Out Cost rate - $91.68

Profit Margin (Profit on sales, not mark-up) - 15%

Bill Out Selling Rate: $107.86

In this particular example you can see that the target bill out rate is $107.86 per hour. How does this measure up to what you actually charge?

You may use a spreadsheet to calculate this if you prefer and test a variety of pricing, profitability, and efficiency effects on that rate.

There are 2 risks

The 1st risk using this approach is that you might not sell the quantity of hours for the year on which the overhead is distributed. The result will be lowering profits because each hour sold will have to carry a greater burden of the Overhead.

Alternatively, having more hours sold for the year increases profits because the increased gross profits will make an increased contribution to meeting Overhead expenses.

The 2nd risk is that, on quoted work, you truly take longer to complete the job than you quoted. In effect you don't recuperate anything on the extra hours. More worrisome is that those extra hours will be displacing hours which you would have been recuperating costs once again reducing your profits.

Regrettably quite a few small business owners and managers don't perform these calculations. Instead they depend on using a bill out rate their competitor charges, assuming that he has calculated his costs correctly.

He may, or may not, have but his costs are not your costs.

Will it really matter? Well, it does. Let's look at two examples. In the first example our client discovered that the difference between his total cost per hour and the actual bill out rate, i.e. his profit margin, was so modest that even a small overrun in time, or improper allocation of costs, would result in a loss on that job. So he wasn't making his profit that he thought he had calculated.

Even worse, in the 2nd example, our client discovered that the true man-hour cost was much higher than the bill out rate. Actually, it was to the degree that the company was taking a loss on every hour it billed out. Even though it wasn't aware of this, the business was relying upon its mark-up on materials and sub-contractors to generate a profit!

Is this an acceptable situation? Should your business's profits come from the mark-up on purchases, or on the knowledge and abilities you bring to the job?

Overall, you can see why people have been concerned. They aren't pinning the tail on the donkey simply because they can't see it. They're operating their business blindfolded.

CHAPTER 10

REVENUE LEAKING PROCESSES

You may, or may not, have heard about Dr. W. Edwards Deming. And, because it's been a while only some of you will recall when everything produced in Asia was regarded as low-cost garbage. Now of course Asian manufactured products have a reputation of quality.

How did that happen? In two words, Dr. Deming.

Here's an excerpt from Wikipedia:

"Dr. Deming's teachings and philosophy can be seen through the results they produced when they were adopted by Japanese industry, as the following example shows: Ford Motor Company was simultaneously manufacturing a car model with transmissions made in Japan and the United States. Soon after the car model was on the market, Ford customers were requesting the model with Japanese transmission over the USA-made transmission, and they were willing to wait for the Japanese model. As both transmissions were made to the same specifications, Ford engineers could not understand the customer preference for the model with Japanese transmission. Finally, Ford engineers decided to take apart the two different transmissions. The American-made car parts were all within specified tolerance levels. On the other hand, the Japanese car parts had much closer tolerances than the USA-made parts - e.g. if a part was supposed to be one foot long, plus or minus 1/8 of an inch - then the Japanese parts were within 1/16 of an inch. This made the Japanese cars run more smoothly and customers experienced fewer problems."

This particular section of the processes in your company is not going to go to levels such as the above, but it's crucial that you understand that it's your company system that creates the outcomes for you and your clients.

Your system is composed of all the numerous processes that you follow in your company from seeking customers to satisfying them, profitably of course. However, are your processes causing, or maybe allowing, revenue leaks.

Sometimes it's easy to fault someone for creating a problem. However, Dr. Deming declared that 85% of problems are brought on by the system, not by the people.

Have you noticed that all good companies have good systems? Let's look at some simple processes.

THE PROCESSES BY WHICH YOU OPERATE YOUR COMPANY

The fundamental concept behind revenue leaks is that they're imperceptible, seeping away quietly and invisibly, depleting cash out of your company. If it wasn't a trickle, it would most likely be a gusher, a gusher of cash bleeding from your company. If you saw the bleeding, you would obviously find a solution.

That's the problem with leaks, you don't discover them until there's a large stain on the floor, or a great deal less in your bank account. It's too late at that time to recover the lost cash, but if you take action you can prevent future seepage.

And naturally in distressed times it's much more crucial that businesses increase their profitability and available cash in their business. This section examines a few of those imperceptible leaks which might be draining your profits.

Here's some sources of revenue leaks:

Failing to consistently evaluate prices against your costs. If prices don't equal increases in your costs, gross profits diminish. The volume of gross profit is essential to your company's overall profitability.

Failure to consistently evaluate prices against movements in the marketplace. If you're not matching increases in the price that the marketplace will pay, you're leaving money on the table.

Selling product lines beneath the real cost of providing the product or service. To put it differently, the more you sell, the more you will lose. I've seen this happen all too often.

Neglecting to recover your costs that are directly incurred against a product or service. It may be something small, but combined they accumulate, with the benefit being that any such recuperation goes straight to the bottom-line.

Remaining in market niches that are less profitable. This can occur with 'traditional' product lines or markets when the market has moved on. The monetary and time effort you devote may not provide the return that new markets may.

Equipment not maintained or repaired. It's not just a slight oil leak, the equipment isn't likely to work as efficiently. And if it isn't working efficiently, then your costs are greater than they should be.

An additional loss of gross profit:

Neglecting to correct recurring mistakes and errors. The time taken to correct an error, mistake, or omission is an opportunity cost, not to mention any parts or materials required. Recurring mistakes amplify the cost;

Failing to evaluate overhead costs for possible savings. This typically happens when companies renew regular expenses such as insurance without obtaining competitive quotes;

Inadequate customer communication resulting in added costs, and unhappy customers;

Poor work prioritization, taking on unnecessary work, work which does very little to provide customer value, or which might be urgent but not important;

I'm sure you can think of more.

Let's look at a single example of a poor process. Some time ago I worked with a customer on an issue concerning service delivery. Research found it took, on average, 45 days from the date of order to delivery of the service. Not surprisingly customers were extremely frustrated. Utilizing a Business Improvement Team with the client, we created a process-map for their delivery process and discovered there were 20 steps to the process.

Additional data collection discovered that the majority of the delays occurred on about 50% of the steps in the process, while the other 50% worked fairly smoothly. The team was able to redesign the process to eliminate the obstructions, decrease the number of steps to 9, and reduce the delivery timeline to 7 days.

Unquestionably the client was much happier, plus much more likely to return. A big win for both their customer, and my client. Then there's the other side, the reveenue leak.

Reducing 20 steps to 9 considerably reduced the cost of supplying the service. Some of that was utilized to reward the customer, but the remainder helped enhance the Gross Profit from the sale of the service.

There was an opportunity cost gain by using the time saved to sell other customers, improving the client's revenue stream.

Undoubtedly you have noticed the other important ingredient to plugging the revenue leak. You're correct if you said data and information. It's incredible how simple it is to plug a revenue leak once you've got some facts about what's happening inside your business.

Improving processes to plug revenue leaks, and possessing readily available data and information in your business, go hand in hand.

MARKET RELATED PROCESSES

Let's look at 10 sources of revenue leaks in back of high level hints.

I found that there's a common thread to the majority of these sources. One way or another, they include the processes with which you run your business? Keep in mind that any business process, however complicated, can be defined as a build-up of costs over time. Poor processes can cause your profits to trickle by accumulating excessive costs (which can include the cost of your time), or not producing sufficient return on investment. Not having any process is even more likely to leak your revenues.

The case study cited demonstrated that another important ingredient to plugging the revenue leak is data and information. It's incredible how easy it is to plug a revenue leak once you've got some facts about exactly what's happening in your company.

Improving processes to plug a revenue leak by having readily available data and information in your business work together. So, in this section we'll look at the data and information that impact two of the processes mentioned. They are:

· Failure to consistently review prices against movements in the marketplace.

· Remaining in market niches which are less profitable than others.

Price movements in the marketplace are best reviewed as they occur in the specific niche you focus on, and I'm sure you target a niche instead of "everybody", right?

A niche market is a targetable portion of a market. Niche marketing is the process of locating and serving lucrative market segments as well as developing custom-made services or products for them.

As Dan Kennedy says, "There's riches in niches,".

What type of information might you need to have to figure out whether you have any revenue leaks in either of these two sources?

Most likely the first thing you'll need to do is to define your niche.

What information do you have available to define your niche? Your own customer accounts make the perfect place to start. Most management information systems will permit you to break down your sales into product or sales lines, and/or jobs you've completed.

That is pretty important information to analyze. One version of Pareto's Law (the 80/20 rule) states that you will get the largest part of your sales from the smallest part of your products or services that you offer. In my experience that tends to be correct or very close.

This means you had better be monitoring market prices on the most significant categories to you, otherwise you're just giving away margin and receiving no benefit.

What you're offering in the marketplace unquestionably forms a portion of the makeup of your market niche, but it's only part. Another part is who's purchasing it - your potential customers.

Here is the part I find interesting. Marketing rejects the view that you should look at how much you can sell (a sales estimate). Instead, Marketing suggests that you need to focus on the customer, looking at the best way to meet their wants and needs, helping to solve the difficulties they might be dealing with. You'll maximize your sales by meeting all of their needs and some of their wants.

Do you know which way most financial accounts are organized? They're organized by what you sell, not by clients. However, it's the client who makes the purchasing decision and pays you the money. Wouldn't it seem sensible to also have the ability to group your clients into their different segments in your financial accounts? Those segments could be demographic, regional, type of client or any other method you group your customers by.

Many clients have to hunt for this information instead of having it at their fingertips. It should be as readily accessible as product or service information.

When you have your customer sales data, you can combine it with your product or service data to more closely define your niche. Try using a simple table or Excel worksheet to track and monitor your relevant numbers.

Now that you have a much better concept of your niche you can resume investigating your potential revenue leak.

Do you have a process to review your prices on a regular basis? How long has it been since you reviewed your pricing in your key niches? If you don't have a process, then I would be willing to bet it's been too long.

Assuming that you do have a process, this type of a review might find that you can increase your prices in one niche, although not in another. Even though you can't raise prices in one niche that doesn't mean you can't raise them in another area. Every penny helps!

Now for the 2nd source. The data utilized to define the niche is sales data because that's the outcome of the buying decision. But sales don't tell you anything at all about profits. For that you need to replicate the table you created above, but instead of using sales data, use Gross Profit data.

That won't be as simple to obtain, but when you set-up the systems to have this generate automatically out of your management information system, you will have a much clearer road map of your profits, or lack of profits as the case may be. You'll be able to determine if you're remaining in niches which are less profitable than others. Sales data alone won't determine this.

A little data goes a long way.

CHAPTER 11

HOW TO GROW YOUR BUSINESS

Business isn't about how much you sell, it's about how much profit you earn.

Picture this - you're being interviewed by the business section of a nationwide paper as a headline item on small business. The reporter asks you about the past year and what you've achieved.

What are you likely to tell the reporter?

Are you going to say there wasn't much difference compared to the prior year; some wins, some losses, the same kind of drudgery, week-in and week-out, month-in and month-out. Long hours and tight on cash.

Small business owners often mourn the reality that they're working harder and longer, but regardless of what they do, there's very little to no money left in the bank at the end of the month. Where does it all go, the reporter asks?

But that's not the real question. The real question is, what can we all do about it?

In my experience an unexpected number of small businesses really don't change from one year to the next. They continue to be slightly profitable, nevertheless they keep doing much the same year after year, confident that eventually they'll end up with a mountain of money in the bank.

Somebody wise once said that all great fortunes come about because somebody took a great risk. I'm not recommending that you take a great risk, but you do have to take a risk.

That's because in order to get a different outcome you're going to have to change something and changing something is always a risk.

To create the story you're sharing with the journalist you have to know your business very well, know what it's capable of, know and understand your marketplace, including your market yesterday, today, and tomorrow, know your business's weaknesses and strengths. You need to understand your business good enough so you can keep the cash flowing with the ebb and flow of sales. You have to be able to delegate the various components of the business you aren't so good at, being able to promote the business and get the most value for your money.

You have to ask yourself this simple question "Why would a client spend their hard-earned cash on my service or product instead of my competitors?" You need to answer this honestly! I see countless businesses claim they're unique, supply a fantastic product with a high level of customer service, but nevertheless struggle. Maybe they aren't so different after all.

Now back to our smart reporter; you're telling him the story of your businesses achievements in the past year, explaining what it has become. Maybe you're telling him about growth. Perhaps you're saying you had a 37% increase in profitability. What did you change to accomplish this?

You do realize that in telling this story you're actually telling yourself of the changes you have to make, the changes you know deep down that have to be made in your business if you're going to break free of the crazy cycle of the same thing over and over again. No change, no gain.

What are the changes you "made" this current year to generate that result?

Dead wood - did you cut the dead wood away from your business, dead wood that's stopping you from moving forward, draining cash and resources that could be better applied elsewhere? Here are a few examples:

· Unprofitable services or products. Of course, you need to know which product/services are profitable and which aren't. Therefore, you need to know the Gross Profit of each, and that it's an accurate Gross Profit (i.e. the Cost of Sales includes all variable costs associated with producing and delivering that product or service).

Do you? Most businesses can tell you how much they sell, but few can tell you where they earn their profits.

Maybe the story you're telling the journalist could include how you create accurate and detailed management accounts so that you knew what was happening in your business and were therefore making informed decisions.

· Unprofitable customers - fire them. I'm serious! Needless to say, you need those accurate management reports again. One client, who had a major customer who was responsible for 30% of his sales, found that the customer was taking up 80% of managements time, time that was needed to operate the business properly. Firing the customer made a substantial difference.

Whenever a business doesn't know how much they're truly earning from each customer how are they going to be in a position to tell which customers they're actually making or losing money on?

· Aged, inefficient, or malfunctioning equipment - the usual excuse I hear is usually that the business can't afford to update, but can you afford not to update; think about the waste, scrap, rework, jobs taking too much time. Updated equipment can produce a significant difference in productivity.

The new equipment could make a nice photo op for the papers story.

· Inefficient processes - the way you do things. Process improvement and reducing production time can produce a substantial difference by, reducing costs, improving productivity, decreasing delivery times, and increased customer satisfaction.

· Inadequate marketing - let's be honest. Many small businesses do an inadequate job of marketing. They rely on Yellow Pages advertising, the infrequent slice of newspaper advertising, as well as a website that talks about themselves instead of about the client and their problems. In reality they're distrustful of marketing, listening to other people in business and trying to emulate them with the same old stuff that fails to work anymore, if it ever did.

Let the reporter know how you revamped your marketing, developed a strategic approach, tested and measured all promotional material so you could determine what worked and what didn't work, measured the return on investment from every promotional campaign, and truly differentiated your business from your competition.

What's stopping you from making these kinds of changes. Businesses can and do grow by initially getting smaller to allow them to generate more profits for growth. Frequently the largest issue that gets in the way of doing this is ego - i.e., if my business is not seen as growing people will think there's something wrong.

There's an old saying - no business has ever gone broke making a profit. Get it?

One more item!

Is there a word that encapsulates the story you're telling the journalist, a word you can print in a large font and tape it to your computer screen? Believe it or not this may help your mindset.

Please read the following story:

"I always had a professional detailer wash my car. For $25 he'd come to the office and do a pretty reasonable job.

But lately I've been driving 3 miles for 5 very hardworking Polish gentlemen to do it. Why? After all, it's nowhere near as convenient.

Well there's the price - at $17 it's 32% cheaper. However, this isn't really why I switched. No, I jumped ship because they do a much better job.

So much better they could raise their prices to $25 and still get my business.

Do you see, better job, great price, excellent service?

It's being much better that matters. And it counts more than having a rock-bottom price.

This is true for your company - for any kind of business. However, unbelievably most people don't say enough about WHY they're better than their competition. Some say practically nothing, or they just brag.

Whatever you sell ... ask yourself: how am I much better than my competitors? And have the numbers to prove it.

Then make sure you tell people.

Maybe that's the message you're presenting to that reporter; that you decided to build a far better business, a genuine business, and you did so.

You finish by telling him as a result of your hard work your standard of living has become better! You have more family time, you have weekends without any meetings or extra records to grind through. Life is so much better.

Now let's turn the story into reality and actually improve your business.

THE RIGHT WAY TO GROW YOUR BUSINESS

Small Business Profitability

I was recently asked, "What's the right way to grow my business?" by a troubled client. Let's call him Jim. There was some underlying eagerness to the question. He was dealing with the normal dilemma of plenty of small business owners - long hours, working hard, and not much money in the bank. Small business profitability is always a challenge.

Obviously, Jim didn't want more of the exact same. What he wanted was the independence of a successful company, he needed money in the bank, sufficient money to take the family for a decent vacation and to see some return on his investment.

In the previous section I talked about the reality that business isn't about how much you sell, but how much profit you earn. Profits provide money in the bank. I mentioned that a surprising amount of small businesses truly don't differ from one year to another. They continue to be marginally profitable, yet they continue doing exactly the same things year after year, confident that at some point they'll end up with a mound of cash in the bank.

To obtain a different outcome demands change, and change is oftentimes difficult. I proposed some of the items that might have to change, such as eliminating dead wood such as:

· Unprofitable services and products
· Unprofitable clients
· Old, inefficient, or malfunctioning equipment
· Inefficient and/or ineffective processes
· Inadequate marketing

It's about developing a better business.

Growing companies share three basic principles:

· They discover what people want and need and make certain they're able to provide them with it
· They have great people, systems, processes, and operations
· They're profit motivated

To accomplish this, Bill needs to take a step back and look where he is currently. He can't move ahead without some soul searching on his company, identifying the dead wood, figuring out the obstacles preventing him from moving forward, and the foundation in the business that he can build upon.

He can't grow his company without constructing a solid foundation. He must have the systems in position to make certain he can meet or exceed client needs and provide a great customer experience.

He has to have superior processes, so he is able to accurately determine their needs and make certain their delivery process knows those requirements.

There's 3 ways Jim could undertake this assessment. He can undertake it himself, he can contact me for a consultation, or he can bring in a mentor/coach to receive an outside, impartial point of view of his business. (Actually, Jim chose to hire me as his coach – but that's another story.)

Where to go from here?

Let's leave Jim, finishing his assessment. Let's discuss you, assuming you have completed your research, and also have your sound foundation.

To prevent a cluster from occurring you're going to need a Marketing Strategy to make sure you have a coordinated and consistent path to follow.

There are numerous ways for you to develop your marketing strategy but one of the less complicated is the Product/Marketplace Matrix. This illustrates there are four possible strategies you can carry out.

	Current Products and/or Services	New Products and/or Services
Current Market Segments	Market Penetration = Increase your sales of your current products and/or services to your current market	Product Development = Increase your sales by offering new or different products and/or services to your current market
New Market Segments	Market Development = Increase your sales of your current products and/or services to new markets	Diversification = Increase your sales by offering new or different products and/or services to new markets

Market penetration - sell more of your products to your current markets. Needless to say, it helps if your market is expanding, but market penetration means conquering your competitors. That usually demands increasing the value of the offer, preferably by adding add-ons or alternatives, and not necessarily special discounts only. It's the least risky, but could come at the expense of decreased margins.

Product Development - you understand your existing clients, their wants and needs, the issues they face. What else are you able to sell them? Naturally, it's preferable to select a service or product that's related to the business you're in now. Your current market is more prone to trust you within the same field but might question your expertise in a completely new field.

You could take numerous approaches to creating new products and services. One approach also uses a matrix. The "Matrix Method of Product Development" has the benefit of providing consistency throughout your range.

What exactly does your client value? The father of modern day management, Peter Drucker, said "this might be the most important question businesses could ask their customers. Yet it is often the least asked."

The Matrix Method helps you to develop products to satisfy the answers your clients and prospective clients may give you.

Across the top of the matrix you have one aspect of the value equation, price. Along the vertical axis you list the product categories you offer. If you were in the coaching business, the matrix might be:

Price: Brass, Gold, Platinum

Product: Personal Coaching, Group Coaching, Coaching Tools

Here's an example:

	Bronze Pkg.	Silver Pkg.	Gold Pkg.
Personal Coaching	$XX per session	Book 10-30 sessions and receive a 10% discount	Book >50 sessions and receive Silver Pkg. + 5 free coaching tools
Group Coaching	$XX per class	Purchase: 3 mo. of group coaching for $YY or 6 mo. of group coaching for $ZZ	Purchase Unlimited group coaching for $XXX and receive 3 free coaching tools
Coaching Tools	One - Book Two - Spreadsheets One - Time Mgmt. Tool	Bronze + two addition books and process planning software	Silver + one-hour personal monthly phone call for one year

Now you have a matrix of three by three, 9 feasible products or services in your niche for your clients to choose.

Marketplace Development - you're confident you know your existing products very well. How many other markets can you locate that have the same requirements? That could mean a fresh geographical market, or perhaps a different industry. Can your product or service be re-purposed or re-branded by any means?

Obviously, the simplest method may well be to address various niches with your primary market segment. As an example:

Adding features, and their benefits, to a product or service to elevate it into a greater value niche.

Removing features so you can offer a base level introductory product, appealing to an alternative group of potential customers who might not otherwise consider your product or service.

In this sense there's a close connection between the Market Development and the Product Development.

Diversification - Some diversification is smart. Very narrow niches can result in filing bankruptcy. If one of those markets were ever to decline rapidly, then your company will still have other markets to ensure its survival.

But that's diversification within your broader market. In regard to developing a marketing strategy this involves selling new products and services to new markets, an extremely different strategy. This is the riskiest strategy, both products/services and the markets are, for the most part, unknown. We understand, of course, new businesses usually have to face this head on.

One last point on creating strategies to grow your business. These types of strategies are not mutually exclusive as this diagram shows.

Your company can legitimately take on several. I've known businesses that plan Market Penetration in year one of a Business Plan, and then Market/Product Development in year two. A great deal will be dependent on your available resources.

Getting to the Business End of Strategy

Having made the decision regarding your strategy, you now get to the business end of your strategy; you must make sales, profitable sales.

Strategic Objective = Obtain a yearly rate of return of xx%

Marketing Strategy = Market Penetration/Market development

Marketing Objectives = Enhance position of present products with present clients, locate new clients for present products

Marketing Techniques = Increase purchase rate 15% by end-of-year utilizing personal selling. Increase sales 20% for existing products through the use of social media

There's no use in just selling more, growing your company means growing your profits, putting more money in your hands.

Now I would like to concentrate on a few Marketing Technique pointers for you:

· Know and understand your client! Remember, you aren't selling to everyone, you're selling to a specific, targeted customer who wants/needs your offering. Figure out who he/she is, what inspires them, and create a specific message just for them. A message targeting everyone targets no-one.

· Some important questions you need to answer: Where do your prospects spend time? Online? Offline? What are their particular demographics? Who are you acquainted with that already knows these people? (referrals).

· Decide your "ideal" client and where they are located, then locate the channels that they're using, then reach out to them and place your message in the front of them.

· Next take it one step further, treat them very well to get them to become your greatest fans. Customer service is vital. Once they are your greatest fans, you have earned the right to ask them to give you referrals and testimonials. They'll also provide word-of-mouth marketing for your business. Keep your clients extremely pleased and not just satisfied.

· It really is all about building relationships, having patience, and providing as much as you can to your clients.

· Remember, growth must be well balanced. You need to work consistently on improving upon all areas. There's no point generating a sales rush without having the ability to fulfill it, or selling a product without adequate customer service to support those sales.

· This also applies to your systems. If you cannot handle the orders, you'll end up putting out fires and cleaning up the mess in addition to creating ill-will with your clients.

· Until you have an excellent product or service and strong systems focus on building a loyal customer base so you'll have some steady, positive cash flow. Then make use of this excess cash to finance growth and expansion into new marketplaces. Plenty of businesses crash because of over-trading.

· Continue learning to enable you to keep improving. Strategic planning, social media, target marketing, customer retention - it's all available to be mastered.

Hopefully Jim will be pursuing this path when he finishes his assessment and actually starts to grow his business.

AVOIDING CASH FLOW PERILS

How you can increase the Cash in your business

Cash flow, not profits, will cause the stress!

Is this you? Research shows the reason many small business owners go into business is to work for themselves, enhance their financial position, and improve their work/family life balance. If that's the case, how has it worked out for you?

The reality appears to be that you exchange one boss for many (called clients), your financial position can become strained, and you end up working long hours, six or seven days per week. I know that's what I found, however I haven't regretted going out on my own instead of returning to a corporate career.

In growing your company avoid the stress of poor cash flow. The reality regarding the financial position of many small business owners is they started their business to improve their financial position, but that's not what actually transpired.

Profit is what you anticipate from your business. It's on-going profits that improve your financial position and build your wealth.

But that's not what many small business owners appear to stress about. Some keyword research tells us that its "cash flow" that's causing the stress. Very few people research words associated with profitability, many research words related to cash flow; words such as 'operating cash flow', 'cash flow solutions', cash flow forecast', 'cash flow management', 'cash flow problems' and so on.

Good cash flow management demands you to know precisely the amount of money that is flowing in and out of your business and is also likely to be flowing in the period to come. It will guide every decision you make. Keeping a close eye on cash is among the fundamentals of business survival.

Understanding how and where your cash moves may assist you in reducing expenses, build financial security, and achieve the financial and lifestyle ambitions you set for yourself when you started your business.

Profits are worthless without cash. Going bankrupt has been the end game for quite a few profitable businesses despite what the financial statements say. This is because the amount of cash coming in is not greater than the amount of cash going out. Companies that don't practice smart cash management are probably not able to make the investments needed to be competitive, or they might have to pay more to borrow money to operate their business.

Here are seven factors which will help improve your cash position and ideally remove the stress in your business.

Improve Profitability

This might seem pretty fundamental, or at odds with the discussion above. However, the way to help ensure you continue to have a positive cash balance in the bank account would be to make maximum profits consistently.

Take note of the words "consistently" and "maximum". I'm not referring to the wafer-thin margins the very large firms can accept because of the volume of their turnover and have formal management systems and employees to constantly monitor operations. I'm also not talking about intermittent or cyclical profits.

I'm talking about you, in the trenches, hunkered down, with maybe an office manager or bookkeeper to help you keep control of your finances

You'll need a good, consistent volume of gross profits. Keep those coming in and the cash will look after itself. You'll be able to pay your suppliers and employees in a timely manner.

Increase Sales

This is a tricky one. If you need more cash, you would think it's a no brainer to try to attract new clients or sell additional services or goods to your existing clients. How often do you see special sales, huge markdowns, clearance sales, etc. aimed at achieving exactly that?

Return to my base proposition - are you in business for sales or profits?

Increasing sales, even on a one-time basis, could give you increased cash flow, but can it provide you with increased profits? Remember, without having increased profits you don't have cash in the bank.

You should be careful with special promotions to increase sales because you could increase your accounts receivables and not actual cash if these sales are on credit. You also may not generate adequate gross profits to cover your overhead.

And that's the problem with discounts. Frequently, when businesses turn to special sales to produce essential cash they offer discounts, however discounts destroy profitability. All they do is teach customers to expect a higher frequency of lower prices, prices which are costing you profit. That leads them to hold off buying while they wait for your next "special" sale.

Or, having bought before a planned purchase because of your 'special' sale, they don't buy later in the cycle. All you are doing is shifting the cash flow problem and offering a discount on a purchase you may not have needed to.

That does not mean you shouldn't have sales, we all need to have sales, but consider how you're going to do it, and the resulting consequences.

Reduce Credit Sales

It's true that making buying easier for people makes it easier to make a sale, and one of the easiest ways of doing that is to defer payment by offering credit. However, credit can be a predicament. Credit customers can tie up a lot of cash.

Some propose that while providing appealing credit conditions can be well-liked by customers, it may also place pressure on your cash flow by stretching the delay between payments in and payments out. Additionally, you need to manage the potential risk of missed credit payments, aging receivables and credit default since each of these might have severe ramifications for your cash flow.

A credit management system can include an array of measures to minimize the total amount of money a company has tied up with borrowers. These may include well defined credit policies, precautionary steps to reduce the risk of credit defaults, incentives for on-time or early payment and installing reasonable credit terms and conditions.

You should keep in mind that you're not required to provide credit to high risk clients.

Of course, from a cash flow standpoint, it's best to not offer credit at all. This can be easier in retail businesses than services such as engineering or manufacturing. You can either request cash or ask them to put it on their credit card.

Another option is factoring. Through converting your invoices to cash, you have access to a fast, versatile and cost-effective supply of ongoing funding which increases with your sales, and it's not capped against the value of real estate. This makes it well suited for funding growth or improving cash flow for medium and small sized businesses.

The great thing about factoring is that it's a self-liquidating option, which means that you're not taking on extra debt, but instead receiving an advance on the money that's already owed to you and in contrast to overdrafts, factoring doesn't generally require real estate as collateral.

Reduce Creditors

Here is the other side of the coin. When you purchase materials or services, you rarely expect to have to pay cash. Without a doubt, some payments have to be made up-front; traveling and lodging come to mind, by and large though you receive an invoice.

Inventory sitting on a shelf can tie up a lot of money.

When should you pay? Typically, companies are tempted by quantity discounts, or early payment discounts, neither of these helps greatly when it comes to paying the bill. It might be better to go without the discount to ease cash flow and make smaller but more frequent purchases, and payments. (However, if your cash flow is in a good position taking a 10% discount for cash, or paying within 30 days, may be the way to go.)

Alternatively, you can ask for extended terms.

Improve Inventory Turn

This is not an issue for service industries such as consultants, but it is for retailers, manufacturers, auto repair, etc..

You need to have the correct inventory on hand to meet customers' needs immediately, and to capture a sale. However, if the product is not selling you've got problems. You've paid out money, and money plus profit margin is not returning. If it is selling you have to be constantly replenishing inventory. If it's not selling, do away with it and use the money for a higher turn inventory item.

The main problem is that not everything sells at the identical rate of turn, or at the same profit margin. A number of items sell gradually; say once every few months, others sell weekly, and some even daily. Those that sell slowly need a much higher profit margin compared to those selling quickly.

In order to avoid the inventory trap good management information systems, supported by management experience, are essential.

The inventory trap is worsened by those individuals who believe it is advantageous to take advantage of a volume discount and order more than is immediately required. Not only does the inexperienced are seduced by that trick, but also those who do not have the necessary knowledge.

Improving Work in Progress (WIP)

This one is not a problem for retailers, however it is for virtually all businesses in which the process of meeting the customer's requirements entails numerous steps; manufacturers, repair centers, construction and some service sectors.

Until the work is finished and delivered, it can't be invoiced. Meanwhile, its accumulating costs in time and materials. The more time it takes the more costs, and money, it accumulates.

An effective program of process improvement is needed to reduce cycle time. This need to reduce cycle time was the driver behind management techniques such as "Just-in-Time" and Lean Manufacturing.

Financing

The remaining large cash void is capital to finance your activities. Companies need financing for working capital as well as for fixed assets. The former can be satisfied, if necessary, through management of those factors above, and financed through revolving credit lines.

The latter, whether its buildings, plant and equipment, vehicles, or furniture and fixtures can create a terrible hole in your reserves if you pay for them from your capital reserves account. Leases or loans spreads the transaction over a period, with an interest cost of course, but allowing you to have more flexibility.

You can do this!

You can grow your company, enhance your financial position and improve your work/family life balance without suffering from stress through the use of better cash flow management.

Management is the key word, don't let the ebb and flow of cash inside your business just occur. Manage them and the stress will decrease dramatically. Your wealth will grow, and you'll have time with your family.

And it's not just cash flow management. What else do you need to measure in order to effectively manage your business?

You need to continually ask yourself these two questions:

1. How do I increase my company's most profitable functions?
2. Is it truly worth it to continue/maintain the low-margin activities?

CHAPTER 12

MEASUREMENT AND MANAGEMENT – WE CANNOT MANAGE WHAT WE DO NOT MEASURE!

If there's a theme that runs through each of the profit improvement guidelines in this book its having the data, information, understanding, and knowledge on which to base decisions.

A fundamental philosophy of management is that all action is dependent upon decisions and therefore the quality of making decisions is a direct function of the knowledge that is applied.

To obtain the knowledge you'll need information, and to get information you'll need data. How can you get data? You observe, measure, and document.

Here are several definitions:

· Data – factual information (such as measurements or statistics) used as a basis for reasoning, discussion, or calculation (which includes perceptions)

· Information – knowledge obtained from investigation, study, or instruction and presented in ways that reveal relationships

· Understanding – the power to make experience intelligible by applying concepts and categories

· Knowledge – the fact or condition of knowing something with familiarity gained through experience or association, enabling reliable predictions and decisions to influence the future.

In over thirty years in analyzing small businesses I've discovered that the most frequent opportunity for them to improve their operations is the gathering and use of information to assist in making business decisions. Occasionally they have the data but are not using it, sometimes they have it but aren't aware they've got it, and in some cases, they've got nothing - a barren landscape from where nothing will grow.

Does your company have any type of systems or processes to make sure that all its decisions are based, to the greatest degree possible, on the appropriate information, data, and knowledge?

If it is important we should measure it!

DO YOU REPORT TO YOURSELF EACH MONTH?

Now why would you want to do that?

After all, reporting might be okay for large organizations, but why would a small company want to do that? I can hear you saying it now, "Why should I? I'm aware of what takes place in my business. Regardless, I don't have enough time for useless paperwork."

It may feel like useless paperwork, but let me tell you about an experience a client had recently. I had worked with this client some time ago. I performed a comprehensive review of their business after which I helped them produce their first business plan. To enable them to keep the business plan on the right track I identified several key factors that would inform them of how the business was functioning.

These factors, typically known as Key Performance Indicators (KPIs) included both delayed indicators (what has happened) and a few lead indicators. Lead indicators are necessary because they indicate what's most likely going to happen.

The system was successful, and our client excelled. They assembled their KPIs collectively and evaluated them each month. Sales didn't expand, or at least not by a great deal. However, that wasn't the objective, increased profitability and success was the objective, and that was achieved beyond a shadow of a doubt.

I also insisted the evaluation be written because that's the only effective way to make certain each KPI is appropriately reviewed. Without writing down your evaluation it's very easy to fool yourself that you understand the implications of the indicator when actually your understanding may be superficial. Your comments don't need to be complex or lengthy. A series of bullet points will work.

It often takes more than a single factor for a business to collapse. In my client's case it had been three factors. The first was the overall business economy (in a good way). It had been frenzied for quite a while and there was an abundance of work. When things get busy, there's a great temptation to set the paperwork aside and do it "later".

However, if you add the unexpected issues to "later" problems start to develop. The first unexpected issue was their foreman quitting, enticed by a greater offer in another industry as a result of the boom in the economy. The foreman was the one who supervised the operations.

Finally, the immediate cause. The Managing Director who among other activities maintained the reporting system, became ill. The illness persisted for quite a while, about five months. One important thing that went by the wayside was their regular reporting to themselves.

That's when I got the call. They asked if I could visit and take a look at the business once more. Despite the business being continuously busy cash was short. In fact, my client was forced to seek a temporary extension for their overdraft account at the bank. Meanwhile they were working hard to revise their reports for me to evaluate.

What did I discover? One KPI in the reports stood out. It indicated that there had been a substantial deterioration in performance in that area for quite a while, in fact, ever since the foreman had left.

When we calculated the financial cost of that decline in performance it equated to the amount of short-term funding they were attempting to get from the bank. Insufficient reporting had been very expensive.

These things could happen to all of us. People leave your company, others become ill. But had the monthly reporting been kept updated the reveneue leak would've been noticed earlier, and it would have been fixed.

There's a lesson for all of us in that scenario. The reports were far from useless. There was, and is, a genuine point to it. Lead indicators are useless when you don't use them, however the message from lagging indicators has to be acted on at the earliest opportunity.

The next section explores several of the KPIs you may want to use in your company.

WHAT KPI'S MIGHT YOU INCLUDE IN YOUR MONTHLY REPORT?

Follow the money!

The last section talked about the advantages of creating a monthly report addressing the importance of key performance indicators (KPIs) in your business, even though it's to yourself. I also revealed the financial difficulties a prior client had found themselves in when, for a mixture of reasons, they had stopped reviewing their monthly report. One key indicator plainly indicated that there was a problem developing. Returning to the bank for a short-term overdraft extension for something that could've been easily avoided was a harsh lesson indeed.

What KPI's might be useful for you? There's a number of issues to keep in mind here.

The first is there are a number of KPI's which every business should report on, others will be more unique to different types of industries.

The second issue is the KPI's must be easy to acquire. If they're too difficult I'm sure that, like most of us, you'll find reporting too hard to sustain. Investing some time creating templates, as well as setting up your accounting system to automatically print the reports you need, will pay dividends.

While one indicator can reveal a performance problem, a combination of indicators may be necessary to determine where a problem may exist. The next few sections look at a few of the areas to measure that you might find useful.

I have grouped these under four headings: profitability, productivity, efficiency and customers.

This section examines financial indicators of profitability. You might have seen comments in the news when corporations have committed a crime, and been exposed, that the investigators "followed the money trail".

These measures are your own money trail. If you do have a revenue leak, then the results will show up eventually in the profitability indicators. Your accounting software should be the source of most of this information, which means it should be relatively simple to collect.

Sales - Nothing happens until something is sold! Business begins with a sale, so you'll need to know what is occurring with your overall sales as well as their trends and seasonal patterns. However, you also need to be able to drill down to your major sales areas, whether or not they are grouped by products, geography, customers, market segments, or pricing. If you're not performing as well as can be expected, then you'll need to be able to pinpoint the exact area so you can find a solution.

Gross Profit ($ &%) - there's an issue here. We normally assume that the higher the Gross Profit percentage the better it is for the business, but in the long run it's the volume of gross profits which determines how much net profit you earn. As mentioned above, the ability to drill down to the next level is extremely important. Good results in a single part of operations could be camouflaging poor results in another.

Expenses/overhead - You will measure these as a% of sales. Your accounting system should already be set up to run this as a report. While you only need the overall percentage as your indicator you'll need the details if you're looking to surface the reasons for poor performance.

Net Profit $ &% - I presume you're in business to generate a profit. Most small business owners are (And yes there really are other reasons). So, you'll want to keep close track of your profitability. Why would you want to know the percentage, (which is again measured against sales)? Well, knowing your percentage of net profit against sales allows you to benchmark yourself against similar organizations as well as yourself. You can be certain your bank manager will also be very interested. They tend to be a little OCD about financial percentages.

Net profit per owner hour worked - In order to calculate this indicator, you'll need a reasonably accurate concept of the number of hours that you put into the business. Sure, I know it seems like every waking hour! Just how will this help? Well, let's include your salary in the net profit and divide the figure you get by your working hours. How does that figure look when compared with the hourly rate you may pay a skilled tradesman, the person who repairs your copier, or maybe your accountant? Does the return seem reasonable?

As pointed out above your accounting system should be able to supply this information except for the last indicator which requires an additional input from you. Your financial statements should not only supply the summary for you to input in your monthly report, but also the underlying detail that will help you track down the revenue leaks, or more ideally, why things are going so well.

The next section looks at productivity measures. These are important since they allow you to compare your business to other similar businesses. Additionally, they provide some useful 'rules of thumb' that provide a quick guide.

PERFORMANCE ALSO COUNTS!

This section examines productivity measures. These are critical since they also provide some useful 'rules of thumb' which provide you with a quick guide as to how well you're using your physical assets. In addition, they let you compare your business to other similar businesses.

But first, what's meant by 'productivity'? This is where we get into a bit of economic as opposed to accounting jargon. And then there's the question of productivity versus efficiency.

As an example, productivity measures are output from production processes, such as per unit of input, while measures of profitability tackle the difference between the revenues obtained from output as well as the expense related to consumption of inputs.

Here are some other definitions from Wikipedia. "While productivity is the amount of output produced relative to the amount of resources (time and money) that go into the production, efficiency is the value of output relative to the cost of inputs used. Productivity improves when the quantity of output increases relative to the quantity of input. Efficiency improves, when the cost of inputs used is reduced relative the value of output."

Regardless of the terminology both are useful. In this section I'll be talking about 'productivity' and in the next I will discuss 'efficiency'.

Productivity measures are the area where you may want to take a look at what is more specific to your industry. Some measures could be appropriate to retail, others to businesses where labor is a variable cost and then billed, such as manufacturers, service repair facilities or professional services.

Sales per person - Divide total sales by department by the number of individuals working in that department. Make sure you are only using departmental sales. You're looking at your operational productivity, not the onetime benefit of asset sales or other events. By measuring per person this can give you a useful indicator of the sales you should be making if you're going to have a sustainable business.

It's also a useful indicator of the sales a competitor may be making based on the number of employees they may have (if you can get that information).

Collectively it could provide an indication of the size of the regional market, or at a minimum the share local business have.

Measuring sales against dollar of wages paid is another useful indicator.

Gross Profit per person - Dividing Gross Profits by the number of people employed. (Any of these measurements, when dividing by employee can be done as the business as a whole or by department for a targeted view.)

Remember to complete this based on 'full time equivalent' (FTE) personnel numbers. There's a concern here which I didn't talk about in the previous section and that's how you calculate Cost of Sales.

For a retail or wholesaling business it's just the cost of goods that was actually bought and sold in the period you are analyzing, plus any associated freight. Conversely, manufacturing companies and those that charge labor for repairs, maintenance, or service, also needs to include their shop floor labor, any consumables, and/or sub-contractors.

Net Profit per person - Dividing Net Profit by the number of people employed.

Obviously, there can be issues here such as if your employees are providing you with sufficient return for your investment in them. It also provides a beneficial benchmark to compare your business not just with similar businesses but also yourself.

Utilization rate - this measure is primarily used in manufacturing and service related businesses. To calculate the utilization rate, divide the hours billed out per person (from time sheets) by the total hours paid.

What you're looking for is the proportion of time you actually recover by charging clients with the time you're paying staff for being at work. The less accurate your time sheets are (are they filled out as jobs are completed or only at the end of the day?) the less labor you will recover against each job and therefore your Gross Profit will be less.

Sales/GP per square foot (total square footage of premises or retail area). This measurement is mainly used in the retail world, this measure is a good indicator of how well you're using your floor space to generate either sales or gross profit. Analyzing these figures against individual departments will give a good indication of the productivity of those individual departments.

Sales/GP per completed job, aka, average sale. This one is computed by dividing total Sales, or total Gross Profit, by the number of completed jobs or number of sales made during the same period. One method of increasing your revenue is to seek an increase in the average sale or average Gross Profit per sale. In order to do this though you have to know your starting position.

Professional firms such as accounting firms and lawyers often find it beneficial to measure the 'per person' ratios on a 'per professional' basis instead.

As mentioned before your accounting system should supply these details except for the Utilization Rate, which requires your time sheets. Your financial statements shouldn't only supply the summary information for your monthly report, but also the underlying detail which may show that a lack of productivity may be causing a revenue leak.

The following section discusses efficiency measures. Similar to productivity, they're important since they enable you to compare your business to other similar businesses. They also provide some helpful 'rules of thumb' that provide you a quick guide to your performance.

What about my business, you ask? If there doesn't appear to be measures here which represent your business talk to your accountant to discuss measurements that might suit your business better.

EFFICIENCY

Get more bang for your buck!

This section talks about the benefits of the third of four key indicators (KPIs) in your business; efficiency measurements. The efficiency measurements are important because they evaluate how well you're using the money you've invested in the business. The greater the efficiency you create the greater the return you'll get for the same investment. However, in contrast to the earlier measures any 'rules of thumb' will tend to be industry specific. You'll need to investigate these for your own industry.

As you'll recall, the last section differentiated between productivity, and efficiency. Wikipedia offered a helpful distinction - "While productivity is the amount of output produced relative to the amount of resources (time and money) that go into the production, efficiency is the value of output relative to the cost of inputs used. Productivity improves when the quantity of output increases relative to the quantity of input. Efficiency improves when the cost of inputs used is reduced relative to the value of output."

Ultimately, it's all about how well you make use of the money invested in your business. What things can you measure and report on that are beneficial?

Inventory turn - Here's how to calculate it. Purchases (from Cost of Sales) divided by the Average (or closing) inventory. If you could generate $500,000 in sales (at cost) from $50,000 in inventory, it would be much better than if you needed $100,000 in inventory to obtain the same sales.

This isn't a simple matter. A number of items will naturally sell faster than others, so you'll stock more of them but in all probability, have a reduced gross margin than items whose turnover is less. What is actually high turnover in a grocery store will be different from parts for a car?

Therefore, improving inventory turn will require attention to stock line by line, along with the sales strategies you utilize to move those products.

Days inventory on hand - This is determined by dividing stock on hand (at cost), by cost of sales, multiplied by 365. This is an excellent warning sign! The correct figure is determined by the industry you're in.

Average Receivables Days - (Accounts receivable ÷ Annual revenue) x Number of days in the year. When looking at this figure you will need to take into account your credit terms. For example, it you offer 30 days credit, average Receivables Days are usually around 42 days.

Reversing this calculation can be helpful. As an example, multiplying the target Average Receivables Days (e.g. 42) by Credit Sales and dividing by 365 will give the level that Receivables should be at, i.e. how much additional funds are tied up by allowing Average Receivables Days to get out of control. I'll never forget the look on a client's face when I was able to advise that if he could get his average Receivables Days down to 42 days, he would reduce his overdraft by $70,000.

Asset turnover - In order to calculate the asset turnover ratio, divide net sales by the average total assets. To clarify and be more accurate, you should deduct any loans made to you as the owner from total assets. Even though the loan is an asset, it isn't being used to increase the return to the business.

The data to calculate these measurements should all come from your financial statement and therefore easily obtained. Of course, to make improvements you will usually need to dig deeper into your financials. Improving inventory turn is just one example of this.

The next section looks at the final of four measures - Your customers.

WHERE WOULD YOUR COMPANY BE WITHOUT CUSTOMERS?

The last few sections have been about analyzing the advantages of preparing a monthly report and reviewing the various key performance indicators (KPI's) in your business to include in your report which may provide you with some insight into your business operations. I grouped these KPI's under four headings: profitability, productivity, efficiency, and customers.

This section looks at the final member of these measurements, customer measurements. Customers are those funny, sometimes aggravating, individuals who bring the income into your business.

Because they are your source of income, it would be somewhat odd if you didn't include them in your report.

Similar to some of the other KPI's you will need to take a look at records outside of your financial statements to acquire some of the information you'll need. An earlier section on profiling customers indicated that these details are useful in a different way.

What useful information might you need to know about your customers?

Customer complaints - what you remember here is part of the foundation of your business.

A formal complaints process is required if you are to have any control over this area of your business. Make sure each complaint is documented and reviewed by you. Besides, if customers don't make a complaint how will you know if there's anything wrong? Customer complaints are among the best triggers for improvement of process, and of the improvements being accomplished. It isn't just the complaint that should be documented, but also the nature of the complaint, including when and where it occurred. You're searching for patterns and trends.

Customer satisfaction - remember, 'good' is not good enough to maintain customers loyalty. Research has shown that only "excellent" will keep customers loyal. This will require some form of feedback from customers either from a survey or customer comments from similar to those used by hotels.

Number of customers - not every business can calculate this. For instance, a retail business will have the ability to measure the quantity of transactions but not necessarily the number of customers. This can be a very useful measurement, especially if your business is executing a specific strategy to increase the number of customers. There are several related measurements below which are relevant.

Customer churn rate (customer loyalty) - once again, not every business will be able to calculate this, but for the ones that can, it's critical. How many new customers are you gaining every month, or year, and how many are you losing. Keep in mind that a repeat customer is worth more to you than onetime customers.

Average sales dollars per customer - what's the average customer worth to you? To find out take your total sales dollars and divide them by the number of customers. For some businesses it might be easier to measure the average transaction value which is total sales divided by the number of transactions.

Average Gross Profit per customer - This one is even more important. Compute the same as above but using total Gross Profit rather than sales.

Customer Purchase Frequency - This is the time since their last order or purchase. This isn't always important for a onetime customer (but how are you going to know if you don't document when they purchase), however consider the benefit of understanding whether a regular customer has stopped buying from you. This is an area where targeted marketing can make a huge difference in your bottom-line.

Customer Frequency - Average number of purchases per year. The more frequently they purchase the more valuable they'll be to you.

80/20 customers - are you aware of who are the top 'few' of your customers which provide the majority of your sales, and your Gross Profits? Be aware that the second list may have some differences from the first. Not every customer will be as profitable as the other.

Certain customers are more valuable than the others and it's beneficial to know who they are. In fact, your profitability is determined by the value you can add for them. Plus, the more you know about the frequency and amount of their purchases, the more targeted your advertising campaigns can be.

The last section brings together all four categories of KPI's and examines how they could be combined into a useful monthly report.

WITHOUT HAVING MEASUREMENTS THERE CAN BE NO IMPROVEMENT

Utilizing your monthly report to improve your profitability

The last five sections have reviewed why monthly reports are essential, even for small businesses, and exactly what key measurements you can include that will provide you with some beneficial insights into how good your business is performing.

This section discusses how all the Key Performance Indicators (KPI's) can be combined into a useful report.

What is a monthly report?

Fundamentally a monthly report is a summary of your business's operations performance over the prior month. It could also be a weekly report, quarterly report, or whatever time period is appropriate.

The report will usually review your rank and progress against your chosen indicators (KPI's) to provide you with a good indication of what's happening in your business and alert you to decisions you might need to make. You may choose to compare the last month's operations to the previous month, to the same period last year, and/or to budget, or even industry benchmarks.

Taking into account your local market and economy can also be useful since this may explain some of your findings.

Why is monthly reporting important?

If you're aware of how well your business is performing, then it's a no brainer that you can improve your business. By improve I mean more profits and more free time so that you're not continuously tied to your business.

Let's begin by revisiting why it could actually be a good idea to invest a small amount of your time in that "useless paperwork" as monthly reports are sometimes referred to as.

You might think you understand what's going on inside your business but there's nothing like a couple of facts to support your thoughts.

In the first section I gave the example of a client who'd stopped their monthly reporting due to a combination of circumstances that can occur in any business, and they had been caught by one costly aspect of their business failing which should have been picked up sooner. It would have been found had they kept up with their reporting.

It's is a bit like performing a customer survey. Businesses think they understand their customers however in 20 years of performing customer surveys for clients I've never failed to find something unexpected that added to our client's understanding of their customers and their marketplace.

Monthly reporting gives you the opportunity to stand back from your company and evaluate what is actually going on. It enables you to discover trends and issues that may not be noticeable on a day-to-day basis, but do so when you look at the whole business, and not necessarily the individual issues.

It allows you to take action immediately on problems that need to be rectified, but should also provide you with an indication of what's likely to be happening in the following period. Lag and lead indicators!

Lead indicators are worthless if you don't make use of them, and the message from lag indicators has to be acted on immediately.

So what will a helpful monthly report contain?

Two issues stand out when thinking about what a beneficial monthly report might contain. The initial one is the KPI's that are included in the report, the second is the analysis and interpretation of those KPI's. Without analysis and interpretation, the KPI's continues to be nothing more than data, and not information. Acting on the information results in knowledge, knowledge about what works and what doesn't work in.

Looking at the first of these problems I said that the KPI's used have to be both helpful and simple to collect. To become helpful, they must be relevant to your business and your industry. There's several KPI's which every business should report on, while others may be specific to various businesses or industries.

If they're difficult to collect, you'll find it difficult to continue the reporting. That may mean creating some systems to ensure that they're easy to collect, but once created it should be relatively easy to assemble the data.

The KPI's reviewed over the last four sections fell under four headings; profitability, productivity, efficiency and customers.

So, let's list these indicators. For a more detailed description you will need to return to the previous sections.

Profitability	Productivity	Efficiency	Customers
Sales	Sales per Employee	Inventory Turn	Customer Complaints
Gross Profit Dollars	Sales per Dollar of Wages	Days Supply of Inventory	Customer Complaints Resolved
Gross Profit Percentage	Gross Profit per Employee	Days Supply of Receivables	Customer Satisfaction Rating
Expenses/Overheads as a % of Sales or Gross Profit	Net Profit per Employee	Days Supply of Payables	Number of Customers
Net Profit Dollars	Utilisation Rate	Asset Turnover	Customer Churn Ratio
Net Profit Percentage	Sales/Gross Profit per Square Foot		Average Sales Dollars per Customer
Net Profit per Working Hour	Sales/Gross Profit per Completed Job		Average Gross Profit Dollars per Customer
			Customer Purchase Frequency
			Refer Customers

You might have wondered why I gave more customer KPI's than any other. Most reports would focus on the money trail. The money is always important, money pays the bills and gives you your profits, however, business comes from customers. Without them all the financial KPI's aren't going to tell us anything, other than there's no money.

Of course, you may not need all these KPI's. Somewhere between 8 – 12 may be all you have to have. I suggest that you complete a trial and find which ones are the most informative and beneficial for you. But be aware of the "lamp post trap". "Avoid using information as drunks use lampposts – for support rather than illumination!"

Some information might be easy to acquire and support the view that you're doing something, but will only provide minimal insight into your business.

Where does the information come from?

Despite the comment above on customers, your accounting system should supply almost all the information. Your financial statements should not only provide the summary level for your monthly report, but also the underlying detail to help you locate the revenue leaks, or more ideally, the reason things are going so well.

For a few indicators you'll need additional input from other sources, and it's here that setting up systems to record and supply the information easily is important. For example, time sheets provide the information for "Utilization Rates". Create a spreadsheet which, when the data is put in, calculates the figure automatically.

Likewise, a "Complaints Process ", which should be a 'must have' anyway, will provide some of the information you need for the customer section. In fact, the 'customer' data is the one area where most of the additional systems may need to be set up.

I'd suggest you compose a brief process on preparing the monthly report. The process should outline the source of information for each KPI. You may find it helpful to develop a "Dashboard Report" which your information is input to a data page and is summarized or charted on the front page.

Also, don't forget the most important section of your report!

You've now determined which KPI's will provide you with a good picture of your business, but the report isn't finished without determining what all the information means. You're looking for ratios or figures that deviate from the norm, or trends that may indicate changes that are occurring.

The data has to be analyzed to determine what is happening, and why. For example, a rise in customer churn may indicate a decline in your service standards, or it may be due to increased competition. In either case, you need to know that it is happening, and why.

Through practical experience this step is seldom undertaken properly unless it's written down as part of the report. This doesn't have to be lengthy, a series of bullet points will do, each one commenting on what the data is suggesting. Follow these guidelines, prepare a monthly report religiously, and you'll find your business results improving.

CHAPTER 13

BENCHMARKING

Capturing the data reviewed in the previous section, analyzing it, turning it into information, and acting upon that information, will considerably improve your business and its profitability.

However, is that a good result? How do other companies in your industry perform?

You probably spend inadequate time studying the most successful, innovative, and profitable, ideas individuals in other industries utilize to grow and prosper. But if you start concentrating on other industries' successful practices, you'll be very impressed at how easily you can adapt these ideas to your own business. Suddenly, you'll see considerably better results from the same amount of time, manpower, effort, activity, and capital.

It doesn't have to be other industries, although that's where the ultimate gains come from. Why don't you start with your own industry?

This final chapter discusses how you could use a great deal of the data you've been gathering for your monthly report for the purpose of benchmarking your business.

DOES YOUR BUSINESS STACK UP AGAINST THE INDUSTRY?

How to take the uncertainty out of growth

When I was asked to submit a quote for the overview of a business, one of the criteria requested was to touch upon how they stack up when compared with other businesses of similar size and/or nature. A great question that few people ask.

Perhaps few people ask that question since it just doesn't occur to them that it may be possible to do just that, and that there could be information readily available which will let them know a lot about their business and the opportunities for improvement.

What they're seeking to accomplish is to "benchmark" their business. I use benchmarking as a tool to start dialogue and education with the business owners and managers. Through the years clients have found it very useful.

To quote one client "The Business Overview showed us that while we made a profit, other businesses in our industry make a bigger profit with less man hours." Benchmarking their business revealed that insight. My client was catapulted into action. Since then they have grown by over 400%.

What is benchmarking?

Benchmarking gives you insight into your business which is unlikely that you had before. If you're like many small business owners you'll have some knowledge of your competitors, their marketing, and their pricing, however it will not be organized knowledge. And it may not be particularly useful.

And also being based on just a few competitors it will not be comprehensive.

Benchmarking is comprehensive, systematic, knowledge about your business and industry. It should enable you to know how you perform against:

· companies of a similar size in your industry;
· companies in a similar location;
· the average performance measures across your industry;
· the top performers in your industry;
· average sales, gross profit margins, your cost of sales, and your overhead;
· productivity standards for key criteria in your industry. Examples include: Sales or Gross Profit per owner or employee, Sales or Gross Profit per square foot, per vehicle, per completed job, per guest room, per dollar of stock; day's receivables outstanding, day's inventory on hand; hours worked per owner etc., etc., etc.

It provides you with the knowledge to improve and grow your company, regardless of whether you measure that in sales or profitability.

Why is this important?

The previous sections discussed the necessity to report to yourself on your business and they examined a range of KPI's which would provide real understanding into the progress you're making with your business, or alert you to possible profit leaks. Benchmarking adds a deeper level of insight into those measurements.

If you don't measure you don't know where to improve, or whether you're improving at all.

Top businesses in all industries use comparative benchmarking to increase their performance and increase profitability.

Due to the fact benchmarking identifies specific areas for improvement it could provide solid ground for developing your business plan and measuring your progress towards the goals you have set.

Imagine you're captain of a football team. As captain, two of the key measurements you will use to dictate your strategy and tactics throughout the game will be the scoreboard, and the time left on the game clock.

And naturally, the more professional the game is, the more measurements that'll be taken. Professional coaches know they have to measure many elements of the game if they are to continually improve the team's performance and probability of winning. Plus, they know the standards they must meet or exceed in all these measurements. Their job depends on it.

Benchmarking will significantly improve your ability to set objectives and performance targets, and to develop budgets and growth strategies.

Of course, some people may claim that their industry averages, or the top performers averages, don't apply to them, but it's hard to see, most of the time, why not. If you decide not to compare your company to your industry, just how do you know whether you could possibly be performing more profitably, or in what area you need to improve? Remember, nothing is good, or bad, until you compare it to something!

In your business would you find it beneficial, even challenging, to know your average sale per employee was 25% lower than your industry average and 35% lower than the top performers in your industry?

This type of finding might lead you to ask "why?" and "What can I do to improve?"

I regularly benchmark clients when reviewing their companies. Every time I do I find some valuable hints which help my clients develop a better, more profitable business.

How do you accomplish benchmark for your business?

Needless to say, benchmarking requires having access to industry data, so where do you get it? Well, that might depend on where you are.

There are a number of sources online that provide broad benchmarking data/tools and you don't always need to be a customer to gain access to the data. For example:

· Breakeven Analysis calculator

- Business Finance Eligibility Indicator
- Financial benchmarking tools
- Comprehensive business finance analysis

You'll know how your business is performing compared to similar businesses by using business benchmarking solutions to benchmark your business, set goals and performance targets, develop budgets, and growth strategies.

Industry profiles and small business analysis provide owners and managers with a guide for profit improvement. By analyzing the top performing companies in each applicable sector you'll be able to see which areas within your company to target and increase your net profit.

I offer a service that will benchmark your business and analyze the findings for you. We will gather your necessary financial data and quickly convert it into plain language reports complete with industry comparisons, ratio analysis, trend analysis, and even expectations. Just email me at ron@afsprofit.com to find out more.

There may also be industry data available through banks, trade associations, and other sources.

Wherever you are I would recommend Googling 'benchmarking' for your country and industry.

Comparing your company to the performance of peers in your industry is a profitable step. It can provide you with an excellent idea of the areas of profitability and productivity that you should improve. In my 20+ years of helping small business owners and managers improve their businesses I have discovered that the greatest single step to improvement comes from access to data and information.

There is an additional step that you can take and that is to compare components of your performance to industries outside of your own. Sound somewhat funny? Well that's where the concept of "benchmarking for best practice" comes from. We'll save that for another time.

PART TWO

Fundamentals of Accounting

FORWARD

Accounting was described by Professor of Accounting, William A. Paton, as having a specific purpose: "facilitating the administration of monetary action. This purpose has two closely similar phases:
1) measurement and arraying of economic data; and
2) communicating the outcomes of this method to interested parties."

For instance, a business's accountants routinely measure the profit and loss for 30 days, quarter, or a fiscal year and post these within a statement of profit and loss referred to as an income statement. These statements include components which include a / r (what's owed to the business) and a/p (what the company owes). Additionally, it may get complex with topics such as retained earnings and accelerated depreciation. This at the upper levels of accounting and in the business.

A great deal of accounting though is also focused on basic bookkeeping. This is the procedure that records every transaction; every expense paid, every dime to be paid, and every amount of money spent and accumulated.

But the those who own the business, which can be individual owners or countless shareholders, tend to be most focused on the summaries of these financial transactions, contained in the financial statement. The financial statement summarizes a business's assets. A value of an asset is what it cost when it was initially purchased. The financial statement also records what the sources of the assets were. A number of assets are in the form of financial products that need to be paid back. Profits are also an asset of the business.

In what is known as double-entry bookkeeping, the liabilities are likewise summed up. Of course, a business desires to show a higher amount of assets to counterbalance the liabilities and show a profit. The management of these two elements is the heart and soul of accounting.

There's a method for doing this; never assume all businesses or individuals can create their unique systems for accounting; the result would be mayhem!

CHAPTER 14

ACCOUNTING FUNDAMENTALS

Accounting fundamentals are often described by the following activities:
· Recording the multitude of transactions that a company (as well as other organizations) encounters.
· Sorting and storage of the transactions in accounts within the company's general ledger.
· Adjusting the account balances prior to providing financial statements in order to abide by the accrual method of accounting along with other accounting principles and standards.
· Issuing financial statements to a wide variety of individuals for various accounting periods such as annual or monthly.
A wider view of accounting will, in addition, consist of cost accounting, auditing, income taxes, advanced profit planning, SEC reporting, plus more.

DOUBLE-ENTRY SYSTEM

Typically, accounting is achieved by means of the double-entry system AKA double-entry bookkeeping. Which means that every transaction and/or accounting entry is going to affect a minimum of two accounts. For instance, paying the rent translates to an entry in the account Cash and also to the account Rent Expense.

Additionally, double entry mandates that a minimum of one account will be debited and at least one other account is going to be credited. As a consequence of double entry, the company's general ledger accounts must always have the total amount of the debit amounts the same as the total amount of the credit amounts. Double entry also makes certain that the accounting equation will continue to be in balance. (The accounting equation is: assets = liabilities + owners' equity.)

TYPES OF GENERAL LEDGER ACCOUNTS

The accounts within the general ledger of any corporation are organized into two major categories:
· Balance sheet accounts such as assets, liabilities, and stockholders' equity.
· Income statement accounts including revenues, expenses, gains, and losses.

Some examples of the balance sheet accounts include Accounts Receivables, Cash, Prepaid Expenses, Accounts Payable, Equipment, Notes Payable, Accrued Expenses, Retained Earnings, and more. The balance sheet accounts are also known as permanent accounts because the balances in these accounts aren't closed at the conclusion of the accounting year. Instead, the balances at the conclusion of the year are brought forward to become the beginning balances of the upcoming year.

Some examples of the income statement accounts consist of Service Revenues, Wages Expense, Sales Revenues, Investment Income, Utilities Expense, Advertising Expense, Insurance Expense, Rent Expense, Depreciation Expense, Gain on Sale of Assets, and many more. The income statement accounts are known as temporary accounts since the account balances are closed at the conclusion of the accounting year.

Once the income statement accounts are closed, the net amount is going to be recorded in the owner's, or stockholders', equity account. The income statement accounts will start each accounting year with zero balances.

EXTERNAL FINANCIAL STATEMENTS

If a corporation issues financial statements to individuals outside of the company, there has to be the following documents:
· Income Statement

- Statement of Comprehensive Income
- Balance Sheet
- Statement of Stockholders' / Owners' Equity
- Statement of Cash Flows

Income Statement

The income statement AKA the statement of earnings, statement of operations, and the profit-and-loss statement (P&L). The amounts on the income statement include the gains, losses, revenues, expenses, and the resulting net income that took place in the accounting period. This is considered best done by adhering to the accrual method of accounting.

Statement of Comprehensive Income

The statement of comprehensive income reports on the amount of net income from the income statement and also additional items generally known as other comprehensive income. Some examples of other comprehensive income include some types of investments, foreign currency activity, gains and losses from holding, and post retirement liabilities.

Balance Sheet

The balance sheet can also be known as the statement of financial position. The balance sheet reports the account balances in the asset, liability, and stockholders' / owners' equity accounts as of the end of the accounting period. Much like the accounting equation, the balance sheet should be in balance. For example, under the accrual method of accounting, when a company generates revenues and allows the purchaser to pay 30 days later, both the asset Accounts Receivable and the owners' equity account Retained Earnings will increase. However, the amount earned will initially be recorded in the temporary account Revenues Earned to ensure that the amount also be reported on the income statement.

Statement of Stockholders' / Owners Equity

The statement of stockholders' equity details the modifications that had occurred during the accounting period in the corporation's stockholders' equity accounts. These general ledger accounts consist of retained earnings, common stock, preferred stock, accumulated other comprehensive income, and treasury stock.

Statement of Cash Flows

The statement of cash flows is also known as the cash flow statement. The statement of cash flows is needed because the income statement reflects the accrual method of accounting, not the cash method. The statement of cash flows lists a corporation's significant cash inflows and outflows that had occurred throughout the accounting period. The cash flows are listed as related to one of the following categories: investing activities, operating activities, and financing activities. The total of the three categories should be the same as the change in the amount of the corporation's cash and cash equivalents during the accounting period.

CHAPTER 15

ACCOUNTING STANDARDS

If all relevant parties in the process of accounting adopted their unique process, or no process whatsoever, there would be no way in which to actually tell whether a business was profitable or not. Many businesses follow what are referred to as generally accepted accounting principles, or GAAP, and you will find massive digests in libraries and bookstores dedicated to this one topic. Unless a business claims otherwise, anyone who reviews a financial statement can presume that the company has utilized GAAP.

If GAAP's aren't the principles utilized for preparing financial statements, then a company needs to make crystal clear which other type of accounting they've used and are required to avoid the use of titles in its financial statements that could deceive the person examining it.

GAAP's are the de facto standard for preparing financial statements. Not revealing that it has utilized principles other than GAAP results in a business being legally responsible for any deceptive or confusing data. These principles have been completely fine-tuned over many decades and also have effectively and efficiently governed accounting procedures as well as the financial reporting systems of companies. Unique principles have been established for unique types of businesses, such as for-profit and not-for-profit businesses, governments as well as other enterprises.

GAAP's aren't cut and dried, however. They are guidelines and therefore in many cases are open to interpretation. Estimates have to be made sometimes, and they require good faith efforts towards accuracy and reliability. You've certainly heard the phrase "creative accounting" which is when a business pushes the envelope slightly (or a lot) to make their company appear more profitable than it could really be. This can also be called massaging the numbers. This could get out of control and rapidly become accounting fraud, which is also referred to as "cooking the books". The outcomes of these methods can be disastrous and destroy hundreds and maybe thousands of lives, as in the instances of Enron, Rite Aid, and others.

BOOKKEEPING

So, what happens in the accounting and bookkeeping areas? Exactly what do these individuals do each and every day?

Well, the one thing they are doing that is extremely crucial to everyone being employed there is Payroll. All the salaries and taxes earned and paid by every member of staff, every pay period, must be documented. The payroll department needs to ensure that the proper federal, state, and local taxes are being deducted. The pay stub that come with your paycheck documents these taxes for you. They normally consist of income tax, social security taxes, and employment taxes that must be paid to federal and state government. Additional deductions include personal ones, such as for retirement, vacation, sick pay, or healthcare benefits. It is a vital function. Some businesses have their own payroll departments; others outsource it to specialists.

The accounting office receives and records any payments or cash received from clients or customers of their business. The accounting department must ensure that the funds are sourced correctly and deposited in the most appropriate accounts. Additionally, they manage where the money goes; the amount of it that is kept on-hand for categories such as payroll, or how much of it goes out to pay precisely what the business owes its banks, vendors as well as other obligations. Some also needs to be invested.

The other side of the receivables business is the payables sector, or cash disbursements. An organization produces a lot of checks over the course of the year to cover purchases, supplies, wages, taxes, loans and services. The accounting department readies all of these checks and records to whom these were paid, the amount and for what. Accounting departments also monitor purchase orders submitted for inventory, such as items that is going to be sold to clients or customers. Additionally, they monitor assets such as a company's property and equipment. This might include the office building, furnishings, computer systems, even the smallest items such as pencils and pens.

PROFIT AND LOSS

This may appear to be a no-brainer to explain exactly what profit and loss are. However, these have definitions like anything else. Profit can be referred to as different things. It can be also known as net income or net earnings. Companies that sell services and products generate profit from the sales of those services or products and from managing the fixed costs of operating the business. Profit may also be known as Return on Investment, or ROI. Although some definitions limit ROI to profit on investments such as securities and stocks or bonds, many businesses utilize this term to refer to short-term and long-term business results. Profit can also be called taxable income.

It is the task of the accounting and finance specialists to evaluate the profits and losses of a business. They need to know what produced both along with what the results of each side of the business equation are. They determine the net worth of a business is. Net worth is the resulting amount of money that results from deducting a company's liabilities from its assets. In a privately-owned company, this is also referred to as owner's equity, since anything that is remaining after all the bills are paid, simply put, belongs to the owners. In a publicly held company, this profit is returned to the shareholders by means of dividends. This means that, all liabilities have the first claim on any money the organization makes. Anything which is remaining is profit. It isn't produced by one factor or another. Net worth is established after all the liabilities are deducted from all the assets, which includes cash and property.

Showing a profit, or a positive figure on the balance sheet, is obviously the goal of all businesses. It's what our economy and society are built on. It doesn't necessarily always work that way though. Economic trends and consumer actions change and it's not always possible to forecast these along with what income they'll have on a business's performance.

CHAPTER 16

BOOKKEEPING: FUNDAMENTAL PRINCIPLES

Many individuals likely think of accounting and bookkeeping as the same task, however bookkeeping is one function of accounting, while accounting entails many functions related to managing the finances of a company. Accountants prepare reports based, partially, on the efforts of bookkeepers.

Bookkeepers perform various record-keeping duties. A variety of them include the following:

- They prepare what are generally known as source documents for the entire operations of a company - the buying, selling, reallocating, paying, and collecting. The paperwork includes documents such as purchase orders, invoices, credit card slips, time cards, time sheets and expense reports. Bookkeepers also make a decision, and enter in the source documents, what are defined as the financial effects of the transactions as well as other business events. Those include paying the staff, making sales, borrowing funds, or buying products or raw materials for manufacturing.

- Bookkeepers also input entries of the financial effects into journals and accounts. These are 2 different items. A journal is the record of transactions in chronological order. An account is a separate record for each asset and each liability. One transaction has the ability to affect several accounts.

- Bookkeepers prepare reports at the conclusion of specified periods of time, such as daily, weekly, monthly, quarterly or yearly. To accomplish this, all the accounts must be up to date. Inventory records need to be updated, and the reports checked and double-checked to make sure they're as error-free as possible.
- The bookkeepers additionally compile complete listings of all the accounts. This is known as the adjusted trial balance. While a small business may have a hundred or so accounts, substantial businesses may have more than 10,000 accounts.
- The final step is for the bookkeeper to close the books, which translates to mean bringing all the bookkeeping for a fiscal year to a close and summarized.

MAKING A PROFIT

Accountants are responsible for preparing three main forms of financial statements for a company. The income statement that reports the profit-making activities of the company in addition to the bottom-line profit or loss for a specific period. The balance sheet reports the financial position of the company during a specific moment in time, usually the last day of the period. The statement of cash-flow reports what amount of cash was generated by profit and what the company did with this money.

Everyone understands being profitable is an excellent position to be in. It's what our economy is based upon. This doesn't seem like a big deal. Make more income than you spend to market or manufacture products. However, nothing's ever really easy, is it? A profit report, or net income statement, initially identifies the business as well as the time period which is being summarized in the report.

You read an income statement from the top line to the bottom line. Each step within the income statement reports the deductions associated with an expense. The income statement also reports modifications in assets and liabilities as well to ensure that if there's a revenue increase, it's either because there's been an increase in assets or a reduction in a business's liabilities. Should there be an increase in the expense line, it's because there's been either a decrease in assets or an increase in liabilities.

Net worth is also generally known as owners' equity in the company. They are not exactly interchangeable. Net worth conveys the total of assets less the liabilities. Owners' equity refers to the owner of the assets after the liabilities are completely satisfied.

These adjustments in assets and liabilities are very important to owners and executives of a company because it is their obligation to manage and control such changes. Producing a profit in a company involves numerous variables, not just increasing the amount of cash that flows through a business, but management of other assets as well.

ASSETS AND LIABILITIES

Earning a profit in a company comes from a number of different areas. It could get a little complex simply because just as in our personal lives, companies are run on credit as well. Many companies sell their products and services to their clients on credit. Accountants utilize an asset account called accounts receivable to record the full amount owed to the company by its clients which have not paid the balance completely yet. Most of the time, a company hasn't collected its receivables entirely by the end of the fiscal year, particularly for such credit sales that might have been transacted near the end of the accounting period.

The accountant documents the sales revenue as well as the cost of goods sold for these sales in the year in which the sales were created and the products and services delivered to the client. This is known as accrual based accounting, which records revenue when sales are made and documents expenses when they are incurred. Whenever sales are made on credit, the accounts receivable asset account is increased. When cash is received from the client, then the cash account is increased as well as the accounts receivable account being decreased.

The cost of goods sold is considered among the major expenses of companies that sell goods, products, or services. Even a service entails costs. This would mean exactly what it says in that it's the cost that a company pays for the merchandise it sells to clients. A company generates its profit from selling its products and services at prices high enough to cover the cost of producing them, the costs of running the company, the interest on funds they have borrowed and income taxes, with money remaining for profit.

When the company acquires products, the cost of them is put into what is known as an inventory asset account. The cost is deducted from the cash account, or added into the accounts payable liability account, depending on whether the company has paid with cash or credit.

GAINS AND LOSSES

It would most likely be perfect if companies and life were as easy as creating goods, selling them, and recording the earnings. But there are frequently situations that interrupt the cycle, and it's a portion of the accountants' job to report these. Variations in the business climate, or cost of goods, or a variety of things can result in exceptional or remarkable gains and losses in a business. Some items that may change the income statement may include downsizing or restructuring the company. This was once an uncommon thing in the business environment, but has become commonplace. Usually it's done to counteract losses in other areas and to reduce the cost of staff's salaries and benefits. However, there are certainly costs associated with this also, for example severance pay, outplacement services, and retirement costs.

In other situations, a company may choose to stop certain product lines. Western Union, as an example, recently delivered its very last telegram. The nature of communication has transformed so significantly, with email, cell phones, as well as other forms, that telegrams have been rendered useless. When you cease to sell enough of a product at an adequate profit to make the expenditure of manufacturing it worthwhile, then it is time to alter your product mix.

Lawsuits and various other legal actions could potentially cause extraordinary losses or gains. If you win damages in a lawsuit against other people, then you've incurred an extraordinary gain. Similarly, if your own legal fees and damages or penalties are extreme, then these can significantly impact the income statement.

In some cases a company will change accounting methods or need to correct errors which had been made in prior financial reports. Generally Accepted Accounting Procedures (GAAP) necessitate that businesses make any onetime losses or gains very obvious in their income statement.

BALANCE SHEET

A balance sheet is a visualize of the financial condition of a company at a specified time period. The actions of a company fall within two separate areas that are reported by an accountant. Their profit-making actions, which includes sales and expenses. This may also be known as operating activities. Additionally, there are financing and investing actions that include acquiring money from debt and equity sources of capital, returning investment capital to these sources, making distributions from profit to the owners, making investments in assets, and eventually getting rid of the assets.

Profit producing actions are reported in the income statement; financing and investing activities are located in the statement of cash flows. Simply put, two different financial statements are prepared for the two different kinds of transactions. The statement of cash flows also reports the cash decrease or increase from profit during the year instead of the amount of profit that is reported on the income statement.

The balance sheet differs from the income and cash flow statements which report, as it says, income of cash and outgoing cash. The balance sheet signifies the balances, or amounts, of a business's assets, liabilities, and owners' equity at a snap-shot in time. The word balance has different meanings at different times. As it's used in the phrase "balance sheet", it means the balance of the two opposite sides of a company, total assets on one side and total liabilities on the other. On the other hand, the balance of an account, for example the asset, liability, revenue, and expense accounts, means the amount in the account after recording increases and decreases in the account, the same as the balance in your checking account. Accountants can create a balance sheet any time that management requests it. But they are usually prepared at the conclusion of each month, quarter, and year. It's always prepared at the close of business on the last day of the profit time period.

REVENUE AND RECEIVABLES

In many companies, what drives the balance sheet are sales and expenses. To put it differently, they cause the assets and liabilities in a company. Amid the more complex accounting items are the accounts receivable. As a hypothetical situation, imagine a company that offers its clients a 30-day credit time period, which is not unusual in transactions between companies (not transactions between a company and individual consumers).

An accounts receivable asset displays how much money clients who bought products on credit still owe the company. Fundamentally, a / r is the amount of uncollected sales income at the end of the accounting period. Cash doesn't increase before the business actually collects these funds from its customers. Having said that, the amount of money in accounts receivable is included in the total sales revenue for that exact same period. The company did create the sales even if it has not obtained all the money from the sales yet. Sales revenue isn't equal to the amount of cash that the company accumulated.

To obtain actual cash flow, the accountant will need to subtract the amount of credit sales not collected from the sales revenue in cash. Then add in the sum of cash that was collected for the credit sales which were produced in the previous reporting period. If the amount of credit sales a company made throughout the reporting period is larger than what was collected from clients, then the accounts receivable account increased within the period and the company must subtract the difference from net income.

Should the amount they collected throughout the reporting period is larger than the credit sales made, then the accounts receivable decreased throughout the reporting period and the accountant needs to add to net income the difference between the receivables at the outset of the reporting period and the receivables at the end of the exact same period.

INVENTORY AND EXPENSES

Inventory is often the most significant current asset of a company that sells products. If the inventory account is greater at the conclusion of the period than at the beginning of the reporting period, the amount the company actually paid in cash for that inventory is more than what the company recorded as its cost of goods sold expense. When that happens, the accountant deducts the inventory increase from net income for determining cash flow from profit.

The prepaid expenses asset account works in similarly as the change in inventory and accounts receivable accounts. Even so, changes in prepaid expenses are usually much smaller than variations in those other two asset accounts.

The beginning balance of prepaid expenses is charged to expense in the present year, however the cash was actually paid out during the past year. This period, the company pays cash for next period's prepaid expenses, which will affect this period's cash flow, but doesn't affect net income until the subsequent period. Simple, right?

As a company gets bigger, it should increase its prepaid expenses for things such as insurance premiums, which may have to be paid prior to the insurance coverage, and its stock of office supplies. Increases in accounts receivable, inventory, and prepaid expenses would be the cash flow price a company must pay for growth. Rarely do you find a business that will increase its sales revenue without increasing these assets.

The lagging behind impact of cash flow is the price of business growth. Operators and investors need to comprehend that growing sales without increasing accounts receivable is not a realistic scenario for growth. Within the real world of business, you typically cannot enjoy growth in revenue without incurring additional expenses.

DEPRECIATION

Depreciation is a term we have heard about quite often but never really understand. It is an essential element of accounting, however. Depreciation is an expense that's documented at the same time and in the same period as other accounts. Long-term operational assets that aren't held for sale in the course of business are known as fixed assets. Fixed assets include buildings, machinery, office equipment, vehicles, computers, and other equipment. It may also include items like shelves and cabinetry. Depreciation refers to distributing the cost of a fixed asset over the years of its useful life to a company rather than expensing the whole cost to expense in the year the asset was bought. By doing this, each year that the equipment or asset is utilized bears a share of the total cost. For example, cars and trucks are usually depreciated over five years. The concept is to charge a small part of the total cost to depreciation expense during each of the five years rather than just the initial year.

Depreciation applies only to fixed assets that you purchase, not those you rent or lease. Depreciation is a real expense, but not always a cash outlay expense in the year it's recorded. The cash outlay does occur when the fixed asset is acquired, but is recorded over a period of time.

Depreciation differs from other expenses. It's deducted from sales revenue to determine profit, but the depreciation expense recorded within a reporting period does not require any true cash expenditure during that period. Depreciation expense is that portion of the total cost of a company's fixed assets that are allocated to the period to record the cost of utilizing the assets during that period. The greater the total cost of a company's fixed assets, then the higher its depreciation expense.

DEPRECIATION REPORTING

Within an accountant's reporting systems, depreciation of a company's fixed assets such as its buildings, equipment, computers, and many others is not recorded as a cash outlay. When an accountant calculates profit on the accrual basis of accounting, he / she counts depreciation as being an expense. Buildings, machinery, tools, vehicles, and furniture, all have a limited useful life. All fixed assets, except for actual land, have a limited duration of usefulness to a company. Depreciation is the method of accounting that allocates the total cost of fixed assets to every year of their utilization in helping the company generate revenue.

A portion of the total sales revenue of a company includes recovery of cost invested in its fixed assets. In an actual sense, a company absorbs a portion of its fixed assets in the sales prices that it charges it clients. As an example, when you go to a supermarket, a modest portion of the price you pay for eggs or a loaf of bread goes toward the cost of the buildings, the machinery, bread ovens, etc. Each reporting time period, a company recoups a portion of the cost invested in its fixed assets.

It isn't adequate for the accountant to add back depreciation for the year to bottom-line profit. The modifications in other assets, as well as the modifications in liabilities, also affect cash flow from profit. The experienced accountant will factor in all the modifications that determine cash flow from profit. Depreciation is only one of the many modifications to the net income of a company to determine cash flow from operating activities. Amortization of intangible assets is yet another expense that is recorded against a company's assets for the year. It's different because it does not require cash outlay in the year being charged with the expense. That occurred when the company invested in those tangible assets.

INVESTING AND FINANCING

Another area of the statement of cash flows reports the investment that the business took throughout the reporting year. New investments are indications of growing or modernizing the production and distribution facilities and total capacity of the company. Getting rid of long-term assets, or divesting itself of a major part of its company, can be good or bad news dependent upon what's driving those actions. A company generally disposes of a portion of its fixed assets each year simply because they reached the end of their useful lives and won't be used any more. These fixed assets are discarded or sold or traded in on new fixed assets. The value of a fixed asset at the conclusion of its useful life is referred to as its salvage value. The proceeds from selling fixed assets are reported as a source of cash in the investing activities portion of the statement of cash flows. Usually these are extremely small amounts. Like people, businesses at times must finance its purchases when its internal cash flow isn't enough to finance business growth. Financing refers to a company raising capital from financial debt and equity sources, by borrowing funds from banks and various other sources willing to loan money to the company and by its owners putting extra money in the business. The term also includes the other side, paying on debt, and returning capital to owners. It also includes cash distributions by the company from profit to its owners.

Most companies borrow money both for short-term and long-term requirements. Most cash flow statements report just the net increase or decrease in short-term debt, not the entire amounts borrowed and total payments on the debt. When reporting long-term debt however, both of the total amounts and the repayments on long-term debt during a year are usually reported in the statement of cash flows. These would be reported as gross figures rather than net.

BUILDING CASH RESERVES

Building a financial cushion for your company is never easy. Professionals state that companies should have between six to nine months' worth of revenue securely stored away in the bank. If you are a business grossing $250,000 per month, the mere idea of saving over $1.5 million dollars inside a savings account will either have you in free fall from fits of laughter or from the paralyzing anxiety and panic that has just set in. What could be a nice well-advised concept in theory can be easily thrown straight out the window when you're just barely making payroll every month. So how is a small business owner to even start a prudent savings program for long-term financial success?

Understanding that your company needs a savings plan is the initial step towards better management. The reasons for growing a financial nest egg are powerful. Building up savings enables you to plan for future growth in your company and also have the investment capital required to launch those plans. Having a supply of back-up income can frequently carry a company through a difficult time.

Whenever marketplace fluctuations, such as the dramatic rise in gasoline and oil prices, begin to affect your company, you may need to dip into your savings to maintain operations operating smoothly until the difficulties pass. Savings may also support seasonal businesses with the ability to buy inventory and cover payroll up until the flush of new cash arrives. Try to keep in mind that you didn't build your company overnight and you cannot establish a savings account instantly either.

Review your books monthly and see where you may be able to trim expenses and divert the savings to a separate account. This can also help to keep you on track with cash flow and various other financial issues. Even though it can be quite alarming to see your cash flowing out with seemingly no end in sight, it's much better to see it happening and put corrective measures into place, instead of discovering your losses five or six months too late.

CHAPTER 17

MANAGING THE BOTTOM LINE

If you do not account for the amount of money you're making, you have no concept whether your company is successful or not. You cannot tell how well your marketing is performing. And I don't merely mean you should know the amount of your overall sales or gross revenue. You need to understand what your net profit is. If you do not, there's no way you can understand how to increase it.

If you would like your company to achieve success, you should make a financial plan and check it against the facts on a monthly basis, then act immediately to correct any problems. The following are the steps you should take:

* Create a financial plan for your company. Determine how much sales revenue you anticipate bringing in each month and project what your expenses are going to be.

* Keep in mind that lost profits can't be recovered. When business owners compare their forecasts to reality and find earnings lacking or expenses too high, they often conclude, "I'll make it up later." However, you really cannot make it up afterwards: every month profits are too low is a month that is definitely gone forever.

* Make adjustments immediately. If revenues are less than expected, increase efforts in sales and marketing or look for ways to improve your prices. If overhead expenses are extremely high, find ways to reduce expenses. There are other companies such as yours. What exactly is their secret for operating profitably?

* Think before you spend. When considering any new business expenditure, including marketing and sales activities, assess the increased earnings you anticipate to generate against its cost before you start to make a purchase.

* Measure the success of your business based on profit, not revenue. Regardless of how many thousands of dollars you are bringing in every month if your expenses are nearly as high, or higher. Many high-revenue businesses have gone under because of this very reason - don't be one of them.

EXACTLY WHAT IS THE FASB?

The FASB is an institution that provides you with standardized guidelines for financial reporting. The mission of the Financial Accounting Standards Board (FASB) is to establish and enhance standards of financial accounting and reporting for the guidance, education, and learning of the public, including issuers, auditors, and users of financial information.

Accounting standards are crucial for the efficient functioning of the economic system due to the fact decisions about the distribution of resources rely heavily on reliable, succinct, transparent, and simple to comprehend financial information. Financial information regarding the operations and financial position of individual organizations is also utilized by the public in making a variety of other kinds of decisions.

To achieve its mission, the FASB acts to:

>Improve the practical use of financial reporting by concentrating on the primary characteristics of relevance and trustworthiness and on the characteristics of comparability and consistency;

>Keep standards up-to-date to mirror alterations in methods of doing business and changes in the economic environment;

>Consider promptly any substantial areas of deficiency in financial reporting that could be improved upon through the standard-setting process;

>Promote the international convergence of accounting standards concurrent with enhancing the quality of financial reporting; and

>Improve the everyday understanding of the nature and the purpose of information covered in financial reports.

The FASB develops wide—ranging accounting concepts along with standards for financial reporting. Additionally, it provides guidance on implementation of standards. Ideas are beneficial in guiding the Board in establishing standards as well as in providing a frame of reference, or conceptual framework, for resolving accounting issues. The framework will assist to establish reasonable bounds for judgment in preparing financial information and to increase comprehension of, and confidence in, financial information on the part of users of financial reports. This also will assist the public to comprehend the nature and limitations of knowledge supplied by financial reporting.

WHAT EXACTLY ARE AUDITORS?

Accountants and auditors help to ensure that the Country's organizations are operated efficiently, its public records kept correctly, and its taxes paid correctly and on time. They carry out these essential functions by offering an ever-wider array of business and accounting services, which includes public, management, and governmental accounting, in addition to internal auditing, for their clients. Beyond performing the basic tasks of the occupation such as preparing, analyzing, and confirming, financial documents to be able to provide information and facts to clients, many accountants now are required to have a wide range of skills and knowledge.

Accountants and auditors are increasing the services they provide to include budget analysis, financial and investment planning, information technology consulting, and restricted legal services.

Specific responsibilities vary widely among the four main fields of accounting: public, management, government accounting and internal auditing.

Internal auditors confirm the accuracy and reliability of their business's internal records and examine for mismanagement, squander, or fraudulence. Internal auditing is undoubtedly a progressively more crucial area of accounting and auditing. Internal auditors analyze and assess their firms' monetary and information systems, supervision procedures, and internal controls to make sure that documents are correct, and controls are sufficient to safeguard against fraudulence and squander. In addition, they evaluate organization procedures, assessing their overall performance, effectiveness, and conformity with organizational procedures and policies, laws, and regulations. There are many kinds of extremely specialized auditors, for example, electronic data-processing, ecological, architectural, legal, insurance, financial institution, and healthcare auditors. As computers make information and facts timelier, internal auditors assist supervisors to base their own conclusions on data, as opposed to individual observation. Internal auditors may also suggest processes for their computer platform, to ensure the reliability of the platform and the trustworthiness of the information.

Government accountants and auditors operate in the public field maintaining and evaluating the records of government organizations and auditing non-public individuals and businesses whose actions are prone to government regulations or taxation. Accountants doing work for Federal, State, and local authorities, make sure that revenues are obtained, and expenditures are performed in compliance with laws and regulations. Those doing work for the government may be employed as IRS agents or in the financial management sector, bank or investment company examination, or budget evaluation and administration.

WHAT EXACTLY IS FORENSIC ACCOUNTING?

Forensic accounting is the practice of making use of accounting, auditing, and investigative expertise to help in legal matters. It takes into account 3 main areas - litigation assistance, investigation, and dispute resolution. Litigation assistance represents the fact-based presentation of monetary issues associated with current or pending litigation. In this capacity, the forensic accounting expert quantifies damage sustained by persons included in legal conflicts and can aid in solving disputes, even prior to them reaching the courts. If a conflict reaches the courts, the forensic accountant may testify as an expert witness.

Investigation is the act of figuring out whether criminal matters such as employee theft, securities fraud (including falsification of financial transactions), identity fraud, and insurance fraud have occurred. As a portion of the forensic accountant's work, the individual could suggest actions that may be taken to reduce future risk of loss. Investigation might also occur in civil matters. For instance, the forensic accountant may search for concealed assets in cases of divorce.

Forensic accounting entails looking past the numbers and grasping the substance of scenarios. It's much more than accounting... greater than detective work... it's a mixture that will be sought after for as long as human nature exists. Who would not want a profession that offers such stability, exhilaration, and financial rewards?

To put it briefly, forensic accounting necessitates the most important quality an individual can possess: the ability to think. Far from simply being an ability that's specific to success in almost any particular field, developing the capability to think improves a person's likelihood of success in life, therefore increasing a person's worth in today's society.

WHO USES FORENSIC ACCOUNTANTS?

Forensic accounting investigative professionals work with financial information with the intention of conveying complex issues in a fashion that others could easily understand. Although some forensic accountants and forensic accounting specialists are involved in the public practice of forensic examination, others are employed in private industry for such organizations as financial institutions, insurance companies, or government agencies such as sheriff and police departments, the FBI, and the IRS.

The work-related fraud committed by staff usually includes the theft of assets. Embezzlement has long been one of the most often committed types of fraud for the last 40 years. Employees might be involved in kickback scams, identity theft, or the conversion process of corporate assets for individual use. The forensic accountant combines observation of the suspected staff with actual physical examination of assets, inspection of records and documents, and interviews of the people involved. Expertise on these kinds of engagements allows the forensic accountant to provide suggestions as to internal controls that business owners could implement to lessen the probability of fraud.

Occasionally, the forensic accountant might be hired by legal professionals to investigate the financial trail of individuals suspected of participating in criminal activity. Information and facts supplied by the forensic accountant could be the most effective way of obtaining convictions. The forensic accountant can also be engaged by a bankruptcy court when supplied financial information and facts are suspect or if personnel (including leadership) are suspected of taking assets.

Opportunities for competent forensic accounting experts are plentiful in private businesses. CEO's are required to certify that their financial statements are trustworthy representations of the financial position and outcomes of operations of their businesses and rely more heavily on internal controls to identify any misstatement that might otherwise be included in these financials.

As well as these activities, forensic accountants may be asked to determine the total amount of the loss incurred by victims, testify in court as an expert witness and aid in the preparation of visual aids and written summaries to be used in court.

WHAT IS THE SARBANES-OXLEY ACT?

The Sarbanes-Oxley Act of 2002 is a U. S. Federal law passed as a result of major corporate and accounting scandals which includes those at Enron, Tyco International, and WorldCom (now MCI). These scams triggered a decrease of public confidence in accounting and reporting techniques. Named after sponsors Senator Paul Sarbanes (D-Md.) and Representative Michael G. Oxley (R-Oh.), the Act was authorized by the House by a vote of 423-3 and also by the Senate 99-0. The legislation is wide-ranging and creates new or enhanced standards for every U.S. public company boards, leadership, and public accounting firms. The first and most crucial section of the Act establishes a new quasi-public agency, the Public Company Accounting Oversight Board, that is responsible for overseeing and disciplining accounting firms within their roles as auditors of public companies. Several of the major conditions of the Sarbanes-Oxley Act include:

> Certification of financial reports by CEO's and CFO's.

> Auditor independence, which includes total bans on certain kinds of work for audit clients and pre-certification by the companies Audit Committee of all other non-audit work.

> A prerequisite that companies listed on stock exchanges possess fully independent audit committees that oversee the relationship involving the company and its auditor.

> Significantly lengthier maximum prison sentences and greater fines for executives who purposefully and willfully misstate financial statements, despite the fact that maximum sentences are mostly irrelevant because judges generally observe the Federal Sentencing Guidelines in setting actual sentences.

> Employee protections permitting those corporate fraud whistle blowers which file complaints with OSHA within 90 days, to win reinstatement, back-pay and benefits, compensatory damages, abatement orders, and reasonable legal professionals fees and costs.

WHAT HAPPENED AT ENRON?

Everybody is aware, at least a little, about the Enron experience as well as the catastrophe it made in the lives of is employees. It really is a story which belongs in every discussion of ethical accounting procedures and just what occurs when accounting standards and ethics are abandoned for personal gain.

Enron began in 1985 selling natural gas to gas corporations and businesses. In 1996, energy marketplaces were changed in order that the price of energy would now be determined by competitors among energy companies rather than simply being set by government regulations. With this change, Enron started to function more than an intermediary than a conventional energy supplier, buying and selling energy contracts instead of buying and selling natural gas. Enron's accelerated growth produced excitement among investors and drove the stock price upward. As Enron grew, it broadened into other market sectors such as Internet services, and its financial contracts became more complex.

In order to keep increasing at this rate, Enron started to borrow money to acquire new projects. However, since this debt would make their earnings look much less significant, Enron begun to create partnerships that would permit it to keep debt off of its account books. One partnership created by Enron, Chewco Investments, allowed Enron to keep $600 million in debt off the financial statements it showed to the government and also to individuals who own Enron stock. When this debt didn't appear in Enron's reports, it made Enron appear considerably more successful than it actually was. In December 2000, Enron claimed to have tripled its profits in two years.

In August 2001, Enron vice president Sherron Watkins sent an anonymous letter to the Chief Executive Officer of Enron, Kenneth Lay, describing accounting techniques that she felt may lead Enron to "implode in a wave of accounting scandals." Also in August, CEO Kenneth Lay sent e-mails to his staff stating that he expected Enron stock prices to increase.

At the same time, he sold his own stock in Enron.

On October 22nd, the Securities and Exchange Commission announced that Enron was under investigation. On November 8th, Enron stated that they had overstated earnings for the past four years by $586 million and that it owed over $6 billion in debt by the coming year.

Following these announcements, Enron's stock price took a plunge. This drop activated certain agreements with investors that caused it to be required for Enron to pay back their money immediately. When Enron couldn't produce the cash to pay back its creditors, it declared Chapter 11 bankruptcy.

WHAT HAPPENS IN A CORPORATE ACCOUNTING SCANDAL?

Whenever a company deliberately conceals or skews information to seem healthy and successful to their investors, its committed corporate or investor fraud. Corporate fraud might involve a few people or a great many, dependent upon the extent that employees are well informed of their company's financial practices. Directors of companies may fudge finance records or mask improper spending. Fraud committed by corporations can be disastrous, not only for outside shareholders who have made share purchases based upon falsehoods, but also for employees who, through 401ks, have invested their retirement funds in company stock.

Some recent corporate accounting scandals have inundated the news media and destroyed hundreds of thousands of lives of the people who had their retirement invested in the businesses that defrauded them and also other investors. The basics of some of these accounting scandals are highlighted below:

Worldcom confessed to adjusting accounting records to cover its operations costs and present a prosperous front to shareholders. Nine billion dollars in inconsistencies were found prior to the telecom corporation going bankrupt in July of 2002. Among the list of hidden expenses was $408 million given to Bernard Ebbers (Worldcom's CEO) in undisclosed personal loans.

At Tyco, shareholders weren't informed of the $170 million in financial loans which were obtained by Tyco's CEO, CFO, and chief legal officer. The loans, most of which were taken interest free and then written off as benefits, weren't approved by Tyco's compensation board. Kozlowski (former CEO), Swartz (former CFO), and Belnick (former chief legal officer) faced continuing investigations by the SEC as well as the Tyco Corporation, that is now operating under Edward Breen along with a new board of directors.

At Enron, investigations revealed numerous acts of deceptive behavior. Enron used unlawful loans and partnerships with other companies to pay for its multi-billion-dollar debt. It provided erroneous accounting records to investors, and Arthur Anderson, its accounting firm, commenced shredding incriminating paperwork weeks prior to the SEC could begin investigations. Money laundering, wire fraud, mail fraud, and securities fraud are some of the indictments company directors of Enron have faced.

DISCLOSURE

Financial statements are the backbone of the complete financial report. Actually, a financial report just isn't complete if the three principal financial statements aren't included. But a financial report is a lot more than just those statements. A financial report requires disclosures. This term refers to more information furnished in a financial report. Consequently, any extensive and ethical financial report need to include, not simply the primary financial statements, but disclosures as well.

The principle executive of a business possesses the primary accountability to make certain that the financial statements have been prepared in accordance with generally accepted accounting principles (GAAP) and the financial report supplies adequate disclosures. He or she works with the CFO or controller of the company to ensure that the financial report satisfies the standard of adequate disclosures.

A few common methods of disclosures include:

> Footnotes that supply information regarding the basic numbers. Almost all financial statements require footnotes to supply more information for several of the account balances in the financial statements.

> Supplementary financial schedules and tables that supply additional information than can be contained in the body of the financial statements.

> Other information may be needed if the company is a public corporation subject to federal government regulations regarding financial reporting to its stockholders. Other information is voluntary and not rigorously required legally or according to GAAP.

Some disclosures are required by various regulating boards and agencies. These include:

> The Financial Accounting Standards Board (FASB) has specified many standards. Its dictate concerning disclosure of the outcomes of stock options is one such standard.

> The Securities and Exchange Commission (SEC) requires disclosure of a wide range of information for publicly held businesses.

> International businesses are required to abide by disclosure standards put into practice by the International Accounting Standards Board.

WHAT'S FINANCIAL WINDOW DRESSING?

Financial professionals can perform certain tasks to increase or decrease net profit that's recorded throughout the year. This is known as profit smoothing, income smoothing or just plain window dressing. This is not the same as fraudulence, or cooking the books.

The majority of profit smoothing entails moving some amount of income and/or expenses into different years than they would usually be recorded. A typical strategy for profit smoothing would be to delay normal routine maintenance and repairs. This is known as deferred maintenance. Numerous routine and recurring maintenance costs necessary for autos, trucks, machines, equipment, and buildings could be postponed, or deferred until a later date.

A company that spends a great deal of money for personnel training and development could delay these programs until the coming year so the expense in the present year is lower.

An organization can reduce its current year's outlays for researching the market and product development.

A business can ease its guidelines regarding when slow-paying clients are written off to expense as bad debts or uncollectible a / r. The company can delay recording a number of its bad debts expense until the subsequent reporting year.

A fixed asset that's not being routinely utilized might have very little current or future value to the business. Rather than writing off the undepreciated cost of the asset as a loss in the present year, the business may postpone the write-off until the coming year.

You can understand how manipulating the timing of specific expenses could make an impact on net income. This is not illegal despite the fact that companies may go too far in massaging the figures so that its financial statements are deceptive. Typically, though, profit smoothing isn't much more than robbing Peter to pay Paul. Accountants reference these as compensatory effects. The effects the coming year offset and cancel out the effects in the present year. Less expense this year is balanced by additional expense the following year.

WHAT IS A CORPORATION?

Many businesses start out being a small company, owned by one individual or by a partnership. The most typical kind of business when there is more than one owner is a corporation. The law views a corporation as a real, live individual. Just like an adult, a corporation is treated as a unique and independent individual that has rights and responsibilities. A corporation's "birth certificate" is the legal form that's filed with the Secretary of State in the state in which the corporation is created, or incorporated. It is required to have a legal name, just like a person.

A corporation is separate from its business owners. It's accountable for its own debts. The financial institution can't come after the stockholders if the corporation should go bankrupt.

A corporation issues ownership shares to individuals who make an investment in the business. These ownership shares are recorded by stock certificates which state the name of the owner and exactly how many shares are owned. The corporation is required to keep a register, of how many shares everyone owns. Those who own a corporation are referred to as stockholders because they own shares of stock issued by the corporation. One share of stock is one unit of ownership; how much money one share is worth depends on the total number of shares that the business issues. The greater number of shares a corporation issues, the smaller the percentage of total owners' equity each share represents.

Stock shares are available in different classes of stock. Preferred stockholders are promised a specific amount of cash dividends each year. Common stockholders possess the most risk. If a corporation ends up in financial difficulty, it is required to pay off its liabilities first. If any funds are left over, then those funds go first to the preferred stockholders. If something is left over afterward, then those funds are dispersed to the common stockholders.

WHAT ARE PARTNERSHIPS AND LIMITED LIABILITY COMPANIES?

Some company owners choose to create partnerships or limited liability companies rather than a corporation. A partnership may also be called a firm and refers to an association of a group of people working together in a business or professional practice.

Whereas corporations possess firm rules regarding how they are organized, partnerships and limited liability companies permit the division of management authority, profit sharing as well as ownership rights among the owners to be very adaptable.

Partnerships fit into two categories. General partnerships will be subject to unlimited liability. If a company cannot pay its debts, its creditors can require payment from the general partners' personal assets. General partners hold the authority and responsibility to operate the company. They are analogous to the president as well as other officers of a corporation.

Limited partners avoid the unlimited liability that general partners have. They're not responsible as individuals for the liabilities of the partnership. They are junior partners who have ownership rights to the profits of the company, but they don't usually participate in the high-level management of the company. A partnership is required to have one or more general partners.

A limited liability company (LLC) has become more predominant among smaller businesses. An LLC is similar to a corporation regarding limited liability, and it's similar to a partnership concerning the flexibility of dividing profit among the owners. The LLC's advantage over other forms of ownership is its overall flexibility in how profit and management authority are decided. This can potentially have a downside. The owners must enter into exceptionally detailed agreements regarding how the profits and management responsibilities are divided. It can become very complicated and usually requires the services of an attorney to draw up the agreement.

A partnership or LLC agreement stipulates how profits is going to be divided among the owners. Whereas stockholders of a corporation obtain a share of profit, that's proportional to how many shares they own, a partnership or LLC doesn't have to divide profit in accordance with how much each partner invested. Invested capital is just one of the aspects that are used in allocating and disbursing profits.

WHAT IS A SOLE PROPRIETORSHIP?

A sole proprietorship is a company or an individual who has decided not to register his / her business as a separate legal entity such as a corporation, partnership, or limited liability company. This type of company is not a separate entity. Anytime an individual frequently provides services for a fee, sells items at a flea market, or participate in any business activity whose principal purpose is to generate a profit, that person is defined as a sole proprietor. If and when they carry on business activity to generate profit or income, the internal revenue service mandates that you file a separate Schedule C "Profit or Loss from a Business" together with your annual individual income tax return. Schedule C summarizes your income and expenses through your sole proprietorship.

As the sole proprietor of your business you have unlimited liability, and therefore if your business cannot pay all of its liabilities, the creditors to whom your company owes money can come after your own personal assets. Many part-time entrepreneurs might not know this, but it's a massive financial risk. If they're sued or cannot pay their expenses, they're personally liable for the business's financial obligations.

A sole proprietorship doesn't have other owners to prepare financial statements for, however the entrepreneur should certainly still prepare these statements to understand how his / her business is performing. Financial institutions typically require financial statements from sole proprietors who apply for loans. A partnership must maintain a separate capital or ownership account for each partner. The total profit of the company is allotted into these capital accounts as explained in the partnership agreement. Despite the fact that sole proprietors don't possess separate invested capital from retained earnings like corporations do, they nevertheless need to retain both of these separate accounts for owners' equity - not just to track the organization, but also for the benefit of any future prospective buyers of the company.

BUDGETING

Ugh, budgeting is just one of those topics we would rather steer clear of, however in business, this is an absolute requirement. To prepare a reasonable and thoughtful budget, an accountant must begin with a broad-based critical analysis of the most current overall performance of the company by the operators who have been responsible for the outcome. Then the operators decide on specific and solid goals for the upcoming year. It requires a fair amount of management energy and time. Budgets are truly worth this time and effort. It is one of several critical factors of a manager's job.

To develop budgeted financial statements a manager needs reasonable models of the profit, cash flow and financial state of your company. Models are blueprints or schematics of how things work. A company budget is, at its foundation, a financial blueprint of the company. Budgeting depends on financial models that are the cornerstone for preparing budgeted financial statements. Those statements include:

> Budgeted income statements (or profit report): This particular statement illustrates the critical information that managers require for making decisions and exercising control. Most of the information within an internal profit report is confidential and cannot be divulged outside of the company.

> Budgeted balance sheet: The connections and percentages between sales revenue and expenses as well as their corresponding liabilities and assets are the components of the basic model for the budgeted balance sheet.

> Budgeted statement of cash flows: The modifications in assets and liabilities from their balances at the conclusion of the year coincide to the projected balances at the end of the coming year which determines cash flow from profit for the coming year.

Budgeting requires very good working models of profit performance, financial status, and cash flow from profit. Developing very good budgets is a powerful incentive for businesses to develop financial models that not just help in the budgeting process but also help managers in making strategic decisions.

REGARDING GAAP

Even though many companies believe that accountants are restricted by generally accepted accounting practices and also that these are cast in stone, nothing could be further from the truth. Everything's at the mercy of interpretation, and GAAP is no different. To begin with, GAAP itself will permit alternative accounting techniques to be utilized for specific expenses as well as for revenue in certain specialized forms of businesses. For yet another example, GAAP methods demand that decisions be made concerning the timing for documenting revenue and expenses, or they demand that important aspects to be quantified. Deciding on the timing of revenue and expenses and placing concrete values on these factors necessitate judgments, estimates and interpretations.

The objective of GAAP through the years is to standardize accounting methods to produce consistency across all companies. But other methods continue to be permitted for selected basic business expenses. No tests are needed to determine if one way is more preferable compared to another. A company is free to choose whichever method it desires. However, it must pick which cost of goods sold expense method to use and which depreciation expense method to use.

For other expenses and sales revenue, one general accounting method continues to be established; there aren't any other methods. Nonetheless, a business possesses a reasonable amount of latitude in applying the methods. One company implements the accounting methods in a conventional manner, and yet another business applies the methods in a more liberal manner. The end outcome is more variety between companies in their profit calculation and financial statements than one may anticipate, considering the fact that GAAP has been evolving since 1930.

The pronouncement on GAAP prepared by the Financial Accounting Standards Board (FASB) is currently greater than 1000 pages long. Which does not include the actual rules and regulations issued by the federal regulatory agency that governs the financial reporting and accounting methods of publicly owned businesses - the Securities and Exchange Commission (SEC).

CATEGORIES OF COSTS

Direct costs are those costs which can be specifically assigned to a product or manufacturer product line, or to one source of sales revenue, or one business unit or operation in the company. One particular direct cost could be the cost of four tires on a brand-new vehicle.

Indirect costs are completely different and cannot be linked to any specific products, unit, or activity. The cost of labor or benefits for an automobile producer is undoubtedly a cost, but it cannot be linked to any one single vehicle. Every business has to develop a method of allocating indirect costs to various products, sources of sales revenue, business units, etc. Most allocation strategies tend to be sub-standard and usually turn out to be hit-or-miss to one degree or another. Business leaders and accountants must always keep close track of the allocation strategies used for indirect costs and consider the cost figures created by these methods with a dose of skepticism.

Fixed costs are the costs that stay the same across a relatively wide range of sales volume or manufacturing output. They are like an albatross around the throat of business and an organization must sell its product at a high enough profit to at the very least break even.

Variable costs can increase and decrease in proportion to modifications in sales or production amount. Variable costs vary proportionately with modifications in production.

Relevant costs are basically future costs that might be incurred, dependent upon what strategic course a company takes. If an automotive manufacturer chooses to increase manufacturing, but the cost of tires increases, then that cost has to be taken into consideration.

Irrelevant costs are those which should be ignored when deciding on a potential future course of action. There are costs that may lead you to make an incorrect decision. Whereas relevant costs are future costs, irrelevant costs are those costs which were incurred in the past. The money is gone.

THE IMPORTANCE OF MEASURING COSTS

Measuring profits or net profit is the most crucial thing an accountant does. The second most crucial task is measuring costs. Costs are vitally important to operating a business and managing them effectively and efficiently can certainly make a major improvement in a company's bottom line.

Any company that sells products should know its product cost and dependent upon what's being produced and/or purchased, it could get complicated. Each step in the production process needs to be monitored carefully from beginning to end. Quite a few production costs can't be directly matched to specific products; these are referred to as indirect costs. To calculate the total cost of each product produced accountants create methods for allocating indirect production costs to specific products. Generally accepted accounting principles (GAAP) furnish only a few recommendations for measuring product cost.

Accountants must determine a great many other costs, as well as product costs, such as the costs of the business units and other organizational units in the business; the expense of the retirement plan for the business's employees; the expense of advertising and marketing; the cost of restructuring the company or the cost of a significant recall of goods sold by the company should that ever become necessary.

Cost accounting will serve two broad functions: measuring profit as well as supplying relevant information to management. What causes it to be confusing is the fact that there's no one set method for measuring and reporting costs, although accuracy is vital. Cost accounting can fall just about anywhere on a continuum between conservative or expansive. The phrase "actual cost" is dependent entirely on the techniques utilized to measure cost. These could often be as subjective and unclear as some methods for judging sports. Again, accuracy is very important. The total cost of goods or products sold is the first and generally largest expense subtracted from sales revenue in measuring profit.

THE COMPONENTS OF AN INCOME STATEMENT

The first and most crucial part of an income statement is the row reporting sales revenue. Companies have to be consistent from year to year concerning when they record sales. For some companies, the timing of documenting sales revenue can be a significant problem, particularly when the final acceptance by the customer depends upon performance tests along with other conditions that should be fulfilled. For instance, when does an advertising agency report the sales revenue for an advertising campaign it has prepared for its client? Once the work is finished and delivered to the client for approval? Once the client approves it? Once the ads show up in the media? Or once the invoicing is complete? These are typically issues a business must choose for reporting sales revenue, and in addition, they must be consistent every year, and the timing of reporting should really be noted on the financial statement.

The next row within an income statement is the cost of goods sold expense. There's three methods of reporting cost of goods sold expense. One is referred to as "first in - first out" (FIFO); another is "last in - last out" (LIFO) method and In addition, the last is the average cost method. Cost of goods sold expense is an enormous item within an income statement and the way it's reported can certainly make a substantial impact on the documented bottom-line.

Other items within an income statement include inventory write-downs. A company should routinely examine its inventory very carefully to discover any losses as a result of theft, damage, and wear and tear, and also to apply the lower of cost or market (LCM) method. Bad debts are likewise an essential component of the income statement. Bad debts are those monies owed to a company by clients who purchased on credit (accounts receivable) but aren't going to be paid for. Just as before, the timing of when bad debts are reported is critical. Do you report it after or before any collection attempts are exhausted?

Not surprisingly, profit and cost of goods sold expense would be the two most significant components of an income statement, or at least they are what individuals will look at initially. But an income statement is truly the sum of its parts, and they all have to be taken into account very carefully, consistently, and accurately.

In reporting depreciation expense, a company can utilize a short-life method and load most of the expense within the first few years, or the company can use a longer-life approach and distribute the expense evenly over the years. Depreciation is a large expense for some companies and the method of reporting is extremely critical for them.

One of the most complicated elements of an income statement is the row reporting employee pensions and post-retirement benefits. The GAAP rule regarding this expense is complicated and many key estimates have to be made by the company, for example the expected rate of return on the portfolio of funds reserved for these future obligations. This, as well as other estimates, affect the amount of expense recorded.

Numerous products are sold with expressed or implied warranties and guarantees. The company should approximate the cost of these future obligations and record this amount as an expense within the same period that the products are sold as well as the cost of goods expense. It cannot really wait till clients return products for repair or replacement and needs to be forecasted as a percent of the total products sold.

Additional operating expenses which are reported within an income statement might also have timing or estimating considerations. Some expenses can also be discretionary in nature, meaning that how much is spent during the year is dependent upon the discretion of management.

Earnings before interest and tax (EBIT) measures the sales revenue less all the expenses above this row. It all depends on the choices made for recording sales revenue and expenses and how the accounting methods are executed.

Although some rows of an income statement are dependent upon estimates or forecasts, the interest expense row is a basic equation. When accounting for income tax expense a company can utilize different accounting methods for a number of its expenses than it uses for calculating its taxable income. The hypothetical amount of taxable income, if the accounting methods used were used when the tax return is calculated, then the income tax based on this hypothetical taxable income is figured. This is the income tax expense reported on the income statement. This amount is reconciled with the actual amount of income tax due based on the accounting methods utilized for income tax purposes. A reconciliation of these two different income tax amounts will then be provided in a footnote on the income statement.

Net income is similar to earnings before interest and tax (EBIT) and may vary significantly depending upon which accounting methods are utilized to report sales revenue and expenses. Here is where profit smoothing may come into play to manipulate earnings. Profit smoothing crosses the line from selecting acceptable accounting methods from the list of GAAP and executing these methods in a sensible manner into the gray part of earnings management which involves accounting manipulation.

It is incumbent on managers and company owners to become involved in the decisions about which accounting methods are utilized to calculate profit and exactly how those methods are executed. A manager can be required to answer questions regarding the business's financial reports on many occasions. It is therefore crucial that any officer or manager in a business be completely acquainted with how the company's financial statements are prepared. Accounting methods and the way they're executed vary from one company to another. A company's methods can fall just about anywhere on a continuum that is either right or left of center of GAAP.

TIPS ON HOW TO ANALYZE A FINANCIAL STATEMENT

Needless to say, financial statements possess a lot of numbers in them and at first glance it can certainly seem unwieldy to read and understand. One method to interpret a financial report would be to calculate ratios, which means divide a specific number within the financial report by another. Financial statement ratios are also beneficial because they allow the reader to do a comparison of a company's current performance with its previous performance or with another company's performance, whether or not sales revenue or net income was larger or smaller for the prior years or the other business. In other words, using ratios can eliminate variations in company sizes.

There are few ratios in financial reports. Publicly owned companies are required to report only one ratio (earnings per share, or EPS) and privately-owned businesses normally don't report any type of ratios. Generally accepted accounting principles (GAAP) does not require that any ratios be reported, except for EPS for publicly owned companies.

Ratios really don't provide definitive answers, however. They are useful indicators, but are certainly not the only element in evaluating the profitability and effectiveness of an organization.

One particular ratio which is a useful indicator of a company's profitability is the gross margin ratio. This is basically the gross margin divided by the sales revenue. Companies tend not to disclose margin information in their external financial reports. This information is proprietary in nature and is kept confidential to shield it from competitors.

The profit ratio is extremely important in analyzing the bottom-line of a business. This indicates how much net income was earned on each $100 of sales revenue. A profit ratio of 5 to 10 percent is typical in many market sectors, although some highly priced competitive sectors, for instance, retailers or supermarkets, will show profit ratios of just 1 to 2 percent.

JUST WHAT ARE EARNINGS PER SHARE?

Publicly owned organizations must report earnings per share (EPS) underneath the net income row on their income statements. This is required by GAAP. The EPS provides investors a method of determining the total amount the company earned on its stock share investments. To put it differently, EPS tells investors just how much net income the company earned for each stock share they own. It is calculated by dividing net income by the number of capital stock shares. It is important to the stockholders who would like the net income of the company to be communicated to them on a per share basis to allow them to compare it with the market price of their own shares.

Non-public businesses do not have to report EPS because stockholders focus more on the company's total net income.

Publicly held organizations report two EPS numbers, except for when they have what's generally known as a simple capital structure. Many publicly held organizations though have complicated capital structures and will have to report two EPS numbers. One is referred to as basic EPS; the other is referred to as the diluted EPS. Basic EPS is dependent on the number of stock shares which are outstanding. Diluted earnings are dependent on shares which are outstanding and shares which may be issued in the future by means of stock options.

Of course, this can be a complicated process. An accountant will have to adjust the EPS formula for virtually any number of situations or changes in the company. A company may issue additional stock shares during the year and buy back a number of its own shares. Or it may issue several classes of stock that will cause net income to be separated into two or more pools - one pool for each class of stock. A merger, acquisition, or divestiture, will likely impact the formula for EPS.

UNDERSTANDING PRICE/EARNINGS RATIO

The price/earnings (P/E) ratio is an additional measurement which is of particular interest to investors in public companies. The P/E ratio provides you with an idea of the amount you're paying in the current cost for stock shares for each dollar of earnings. Earnings prop up the marketplace value of stock shares, not the book value of the stock shares that is reported in the balance sheet.

The P/E ratio can be a reality check on precisely how high the current market price is in relation to the underlying profit that the company is earning. Extremely high P/E ratios are warranted only if investors believe that the business's earnings per share (EPS) provides extensive upside potential in the future.

The P/E ratio is calculated dividing the present market price of the stock by the most current trailing 12 months diluted EPS. Stock share prices jump around every day and tend to be subject to big variations on short notice. The current P/E ratio really should be compared to the average stock market P/E to evaluate whether the company is selling below or above the market average.

P/E ratios differ from industry to industry and from year to year. One dollar of EPS may command a $10 market value for a mature business in a no-growth industry, while a dollar of EPS in a dynamic business in a growth industry could have a $30 market value per dollar of earnings, or net income.

To sum it up, the price/earnings ratio, or P/E ratio is the current market price of a capital stock divided by its trailing 12 months' diluted earnings per share (EPS) or its basic earnings per share if the business doesn't report diluted EPS. A lower P/E may indicate an undervalued stock or a cynical forecast by investors. A higher P/E may expose an overvalued stock or could be based on a confident forecast by investors.

WHAT'S THE DIFFERENCE BETWEEN PUBLIC AND PRIVATE ORGANIZATION REPORTING?

A public corporation is a company whose securities are exchanged on the public stock exchanges, such as the New York Stock Exchange as well as Nasdaq. A private business is held solely by its owners and isn't traded publicly. Whenever the shareholders of a private organization receive the periodical financial reports, they're entitled to assume that the business's financial statements and footnotes are prepared in agreement with GAAP. Otherwise, the president or chief officer of the company should clearly advise the shareholders that GAAP weren't followed in one or more aspects. The information of a private company's annual financial report is usually minimal. It consists of the three primary financial statements - the balance sheet, income statement and statement of cash flows. There's normally no letter from the chief executive officer, no photos, and no diagrams.

On the other hand, the annual report of a publicly traded company has more features to it. Additionally, there are more requirements for reporting. Included in this are the management discussion and analysis (MD&A) section that presents the top managers' understanding and analysis of the company's profit performance and additional important financial developments within the year.

Another section required for public organizations is the earnings per share (EPS). This is the sole ratio that a public business is required to report although most public organizations report a few others as well. A three-year comparative income statement is also likely required.

Quite a few publicly owned organizations make their required filings with the SEC, however they present completely different annual financial reports to their stockholders. A great deal of public businesses includes only condensed financial information instead of comprehensive financial statements. They'll normally refer the reader to a more detailed SEC financial report for additional specifics.

WHAT ARE ADDITIONAL RATIOS UTILIZED IN FINANCIAL REPORTING?

The dividend yield ratio informs investors how much cash income they are acquiring on their own stock investment in a company. This is determined by dividing the annual cash dividend per share by the current market price of the stock. This may be compared to the interest rate on high-grade debt securities that pay out interest, such as Treasure bonds and Treasury notes, which are considered among the safest.

Book value per share is calculated by dividing total owners' equity by the total number of stock shares which are outstanding. While EPS is much more important to determine the market value of a stock book value per share is a way of measuring the documented value of the business's assets less its liabilities, which equals the net assets which are backing up the business's stock shares. It's a possibility that the market value associated with a stock could be less than the book value per share.

The return on equity (ROE) ratio tells exactly how much profit a company earned as compared to the book value of its stockholders' equity. This particular ratio is particularly useful for privately owned companies, which don't have a way of determining the current value of owners' equity. ROE is additionally calculated for public companies, but it plays a secondary role compared to other ratios. ROE is calculated by dividing net income by owners' equity.

The current ratio is a way of measuring a company's short-term solvency. In other words, its capability to pay its liabilities which come due in the near future. This ratio is an estimated indication of whether cash on hand as well as the cash to be collected from accounts receivable and from selling inventory is going to be enough to pay off the liabilities which will come due over the following period. It is calculated by dividing the current assets by the current liabilities. Companies are expected to maintain a minimum 2 to 1 current ratio, meaning its current assets needs to be twice its current liabilities.

DISCOVER THE ACID TEST RATIO AND ROA RATIO.

Investors calculate the acid test ratio, also referred to as the quick ratio, as well as the pounce ratio. This ratio excludes inventory and prepaid expenses, which the current ratio includes, and it also limits assets to cash and items which the company can quickly convert to cash. This constrained category of assets is referred to as quick or liquid assets. The acid-test ratio is computed by dividing the liquid assets by the total current liabilities.

This ratio is likewise known as the pounce ratio to emphasize that you have calculated for a worst-case scenario where the company's creditors could pounce on the company and demand prompt payment of the company's liabilities. Short-term creditors don't have the legal right to demand immediate payment, except for unusual circumstances. This ratio is a conservative method to look at a company's capacity to pay its short-term liabilities.

One component that affects the bottom-line profitability of a company is whether or not it uses debt to its benefit. A company may realize a financial leverage gain, which means it earns more profit on the money it has borrowed versus the interest paid for the use of the borrowed money. A substantial portion of a company's net income for the year may be due to financial leverage. The ROA ratio is calculated by dividing the earnings before interest and income tax (EBIT) by the net operating assets.

An investor compares the ROA with the interest rate which the organization borrowed money. If a business's ROA is 14 percent and the interest rate on its debt is 8 percent, the company's net gain on its capital is 6 percent more than what it is paying in interest.

ROA is a helpful ratio for interpreting profit performance, apart from determining financial gain or loss. ROA is referred to as a capital utilization test that measures how profit before interest and income tax was earned on the total capital used by the business.

WHAT EXACTLY ARE INDEPENDENT AUDITORS?

Independent CPA auditors are similar to referees within the financial reporting arena. The CPA arrives, performs an audit of the company's accounting system and methods and provides a report which is attached to the company's financial statements. Publicly owned companies are required to have their own annual financial reports audited by independent CPA firms as well as some privately-owned companies who have audits done because they realize that an audit report will add trustworthiness to their financial reports.

An auditor judges whether the company's accounting methods are in compliance with generally accepted accounting principles (GAAP). Normally everything is in place and the financial report is a reliable document. However, sometimes an auditor will wave a yellow or red flag. Several indicators of potential trouble include when the company's capability to proceed with regular operations is in question due to what are referred to as financial exigencies, that may mean a small cash balance, past due liabilities, or major lawsuits that the company does not have the money to cover.

An auditor must exercise professional skepticism, meaning that the auditor should contest the accounting strategies and reporting practices of the client in order to ensure that its financial statement conform with accounting standards and aren't misleading. In short, that the financial statement is fairly presented. In fact, the words "fairly presented" are the precise words used in the auditor's report.

An effective auditor needs technical knowledge, but in addition must understand how to be tough on the accounting strategies to the client. His / her job is to be the representative of the stockholders and other people that use the company's financial statement. It is incumbent on an auditor to strictly uphold GAAP and never let any irregularities slide.

There are numerous well-known businesses that engaged in accounting fraud lately and that fraud wasn't discovered by the CPA auditors. Enron is among these businesses. In this case, the auditing firm, Arthur Anderson was found to be guilty of obstruction of justice due to the fact it destroyed audit evidence.

WHAT DO THEY MEAN BY ACCOUNTING FRAUD?

Accounting fraud is a planned and inappropriate manipulation of the documenting of revenue and/or expenses in order to make a business's profit performance appear more favorable than it actually is. Several things which businesses do that can constitute fraud are:

> Not documenting prepaid expenses or various other incidental assets.
> Not displaying specific classifications of current assets and/or liabilities.
> Combining short and long-term debt into one amount.

Over-recording sales revenue is considered the most common method of accounting fraud. A company might ship products to customers that the customer has not ordered, fully understanding those customers will return the products following the end of the year. Until the returns are made, the company records the shipments as though they had been actual sales. Or a business may participate in channel stuffing. It delivers products to retailers or the ultimate consumers that they really don't want, but business's make deals privately that offer incentives and exclusive privileges if the retailers or customers won't object to taking earlier delivery of the products. A company might also postpone recording products that have been returned by customers to avoid acknowledging these offsets against sales revenue in the present year.

Another way a company commits accounting fraud can be by under-recording expenses, for instance, not recording depreciation expense. Or maybe a company might choose to not record all its cost of goods sold expense for the sales created during a period. This would result in the gross margin being higher though the company's inventory asset would include products that aren't in inventory due to the fact they've been delivered to customers.

A company may also choose to not record asset losses that should be recognized, for instance, uncollectible accounts receivable, or it may not write down inventory under the lower of cost or market rule. A company could also not record the entire amount of the liability for an expense, causing that liability to be understated in the company's balance sheet. Its profit, consequently, would be overstated.

WHAT IS THE PURPOSE OF AN AUDIT?

If a company breaks the rules of accounting and ethics, it may be accountable for legal sanctions against it. It can intentionally mislead their investors and lenders with fictitious or misleading numbers in their financial report. This is where audits come in. Audits are one way of keeping deceptive financial reporting to a minimum. CPA auditors are similar to highway patrol officers who enforce traffic laws and regulations and issue tickets to help keep speeding to a minimum. An audit examination can expose problems that the company wasn't aware of.

After finishing an audit examination, the CPA prepares a brief report saying that the company has prepared its financial statements, in accordance with generally accepted accounting principles (GAAP), or where it has not. All companies which are publicly traded are required to have yearly audits by independent CPA's. Those businesses whose stocks are listed on the New York Stock Exchange or Nasdaq have to be audited by outside CPA firms. For a publicly traded company, the cost of conducting a yearly audit is the cost of doing business; it is the price a company will pay for going into public markets for their capital and for having its shares traded in the public venue.

Even though federal law doesn't demand audits for private companies, financial institutions and other lenders to private companies might insist on audited financial statements. If the lenders do not require audited statements, a business's owners must choose whether an audit is a good investment. Rather than an audit which they cannot really afford, quite a few smaller businesses have an outside CPA come in on a regular basis to review their accounting methods and provide advice on their financial reporting. But unless a CPA has completed an audit, he / she should be cautious not to express an opinion of the financial statements. Without having a careful examination of the data supporting the amounts reported in the financial statements, the CPA is in no position to supply an opinion on the financial statements prepared from the accounts of the company.

WHAT DOES AN AUDIT REPORT CONTAIN?

Most audit reports on financial statements provide the company a clean bill of health, or a clean opinion. At the opposite end of the spectrum, the auditor may state that the financial statements are misleading and shouldn't be relied upon. This unfavorable audit report is called an adverse opinion. That's the big stick that auditors carry. They've got the ability to give a company's financial statements an adverse opinion, and no company wants that. The threat of a detrimental opinion more often than not motivates a company to give way to the auditor and alter its accounting or disclosure to prevent getting the kiss of death of an adverse opinion. An adverse audit opinion states that the financial statements of the company are misleading. The SEC won't tolerate adverse opinions by auditors of public businesses; it would suspend trading in a company's stock if the company received an adverse opinion from the CPA auditor.

One modification to an auditor's report is extremely significant – when the CPA firm states that it has considerable concerns about the capability of the company to continue as a going concern. A going concern is a business that has adequate financial wherewithal and momentum to carry on its regular operations into the foreseeable future and will be able to absorb a negative turn of events without needing to default on its liabilities. A going concern won't face an impending financial crisis or any demanding financial emergency. A company might be under some financial distress but overall still be judged a going concern. Except when there is evidence to the contrary, the CPA auditor assumes that the company is a going concern. If an auditor has significant concerns about whether or not the company is a going concern, these concerns are detailed in the auditor's report.

HOW ACCOUNTING IS USED IN BUSINESS?

It may appear obvious, however in managing a company, it's important to understand how the company generates a profit. A company needs an effective business model and a great profit model. A business sells services or products and earns an amount of margin on each unit sold. The quantity of units sold is the sales volume during the reporting period. The company subtracts the amount of fixed expenses for the time period which provides them with the operating profit before interest and income tax.

It is very important to not confuse profit with cash flow. Profit equates to sales revenue minus expenses. A business manager should not assume that sales revenue is equal to cash inflow and that expenses equal cash outflows. In recording sales revenue, cash or many other assets, are increased. The asset accounts receivable, is increased in documenting revenue for sales made on credit. Quite a few expenses are recorded by decreasing an asset other than cash. For instance, cost of goods sold is recorded along with a decrease to the inventory asset as well as depreciation expense is recorded with a decrease to the book value of fixed assets. Additionally, some expenses are recorded with an increase in the accounts payable liability or an increase in the accrued expenses payable liability.

Keep in mind that some budgeting is better than none. Budgeting provides important benefits, like understanding the profit characteristics and the financial framework of the business. It also helps for planning for fluctuations in the upcoming reporting period. Budgeting forces a business manager to target the factors which need to be improved upon to help increase profit. A well-designed management profit-and-loss report supplies the essential framework for budgeting profit. It is advisable to look ahead to the coming year. Regardless of anything else, at least input the figures in your profit report for sales volume, sales prices, product costs, along with other expenses and see how your forecasted profit looks for the coming year.

SOME ADDITIONAL TOOLS TO HELP YOU.

Contact us for current pricing on any of these tools, or any questions you may have, at ron@afsprofit.com

FORENSIC DIAGNOSTIC

Do I hear you say, "But I need more than that?" The Forensic Diagnostic is where I work with you to drill down further into your business, looking for telltale clues which may guide us to the profit leak.

The Forensic Diagnostic comes to you as a workbook which guides you through a series of questions and tables for you to complete.

When you return the workbook, I analyze the results and prepare a practical report on the issues I identify and make specific, practical recommendations on the steps you may take to plug the profit leak. If required I will contact you by telephone or email to clarify any areas of your response.

Bonus–once you have received the report I will have a one-to-one conference call (1 hour) to discuss our findings and the rationale for our recommendations.

DASHBOARD MONTHLY REPORT

This book emphasized the need to measure and report. How do you know that there has been a profit leak?

When the clues in the figures tell you!

Time and time again I have had clients tell me that if only they had known earlier that there was a problem they could have done something about it. But they couldn't see the clues that would have alerted them because they didn't collect their business data into one spot and report on it.

If you don't know you have a problem, or you don't know where the problem is, you can't fix it.

To meet that need I developed the AFS Profit Leak Dashboard Report. It will help you identify just where things might not be working as well as they could, or should, through a graphical interpretation of your key financial and other indicators. All graphs are on one page to enable you to see and assess the condition of your business at a glance.

SLIGHT CHANGES = BIG RESULTS - HOW TO DRAMATICALLY IMPROVE YOUR QUOTES & PROPOSALS

Quotes and proposals are fundamental to so many types of businesses. As you will see in this manual, many are done very badly and leave the customer with only one thing on which they make their decision - price.

But you know when you purchase something you take into consideration many other things.

Small Changes = Big Results will enable you to bring those considerations into play the next time you prepare a quotation or proposal. The lowest price doesn't always have to win.

You CAN remove price from the decision process by following the steps in this book. It provides a template on which to build your next proposal or quotation.

You know the value of your average sale, and your proposal success rate. What would be the impact on your bottom line if you could increase your proposal success rate from, say, 30% to 40%?

This manual provides expert guidance on how to do so. Even just one more successful proposal will more than repay this investment.

Format: pdf document + MP3 to listen to in the car or out exercising

10 TOOLS TO INCREASE SALES

You probably started your business because you are good at what you do. To be good at what you do, you've had to spend quite a bit of time learning your profession or trade.

One skill you probably had little opportunity to study and learn is selling; how to get sales. Yet winning sales is the lifeblood of your business. For your business to succeed and provide you profit, you need to put the same time and effort into learning how to increase sales, to keep customers coming through your door.

Format: It comes as an e-book (pdf), plus MP3 to listen to in the car or out exercising.

Please make sure to check out our membership site specifically for small business at afsprofit.com.

If you have any questions or comments about this book or our services, please contact us at support@afsprofit.com.

NEVER buy anything without a guarantee!

Our guarantee is simple. If you are not satisfied return the product within 30 days and we will refund 100% of your price. No hassles, no issues.

To your continued success,
Ron

ABOUT RON VEST

I have been supporting small and medium size enterprises for over 30 years as a business leader, coach, and management consultant. To do so I draw upon my many years' experience at senior management levels. This experience includes manufacturing, professional services, retail, logistics, and management consulting, with responsibilities in all aspects of growing a profitable company.

Managing a small business is not always easy. Do you:

· Struggle with cash flow, profitability, and available management time.

· Know you work hard and are a good operator in your area of business; but

· Find that, because you are always busy, you lack the time to identify the key constraints on you and your business.

· Suffer from profit leaks in the business which drain the profits you hope for.

· As a result, you work long hours, seven days a week and rarely have the time to enjoy what you do.

If this is you, then you are the type of small business that AFS Profit assists.

Some people promise solutions – we provide results!

If you are a typical business owner, you started your business because you are good at what you do, and that has gotten you to where you are today. But to keep building your business you may need guidance or assistance in areas in which you haven't had the time or opportunity to develop expertise. For most small and medium size businesses these may be developing a clear strategic direction, developing effective management systems and processes, understanding financial management, or how to effectively market your business.

Do you recognize yourself above – an owner operator who has built a business based on your expertise but find yourself struggling with cash flow, profitability and never enough time? That's where I specialize, helping small and medium size businesses overcome these burdens.

Of course, I don't know your business as well you do; nobody does, and it would be egotistical of me to suggest otherwise. What I do bring is knowledge of techniques and principles to find and fix areas of profit loss which can be applied widely to small businesses. I have successfully worked with businesses across a wide range of industries, from tourism to real estate, IT, engineering and manufacturing and each time I have been able to identify opportunities for improvement which had a positive impact on the business.

Many years of practical experience in business, hands-on direct management experience, and running a small business enables me to bring to you a deep understanding of how small business should operate and the pressures you face.

I specialize in working with small businesses because I understand the issues they face, the need to have greater control over their business, and to improve their quality of life. Please feel free to reach me at ron@afsprofit.com or join me on Facebook at facebook.com/smallbusinesschamp/. I would love to hear from you!!!!!!

www.ingramcontent.com/pod-product-compliance
Lightning Source LLC
Chambersburg PA
CBHW070241230526
45470CB00002B/470